My Name Is Ruth

2.0

God bless you!

Patricia Sutton Burgess
10/4/15

Phil 1:3

By

Patricia Sutton Burgess

1

Printed by Create Space, An Amazon.com Company

ISBN: 13: 978-1508834649

  10: 1508834644

Cover Picture: Charlaine Hester

Cover Feature: Friendship Baptist Church, Hiawassee, GA

Cover Design: Fiver, by Jimmy Gibbs, Designer58

Friendship Baptist Church was built, in part by my Grandfather and Great-grandfather Sutton. My father was baptized here at age 12. When he married my mother, she was Methodist, so she was baptized here in the same river. I attended church here as a girl.

Dedication

In the memory of my son Michael and in honor my children, Mark and Charlaine, who lived most of this with me, and with whom I share today the vision of Ruth and living close to God.

Dedicated to the memory of the man whom I married, whose love made me a Ruth, and whom I shall meet again in eternity.

And, in honor the dear, dear, people who made up the congregations of every church we served: Camak, Pearlington, Nicholls, Unadilla, Twin City, Covington, Cobbtown, and Lithia Springs. What marvelous lessons you taught me.

Finally, in honor the ladies of the Esther Sunday School Class of the McConnell Memorial Baptist Church in Hiawassee, Georgia, Laverne, Barbara, Georgia, Brenda A, Brenda P, Janie, Betty P, Lottie, Mozelle, Ophelia, Ellen H, Ellen M, Sara A, Sara H, Teresa, Joyce, Manita, Anne, Ina, Ruth, Marie, Modean, Kathy, and Pat, all of whom have accepted me as one of them, loved me, cried with me, rejoiced with me, supported me and my efforts, and walk with me every day in the path God leads us.

Table of Contents

Prologue

In 1979, I published a book entitled *My Name Is Ruth* which was well accepted. At that time, I was forty five years old, having been a Pastor's wife for twenty five years with three children—two in high school and one in middle school. I was just ready to graduate from college and thinking about a career teaching high school. Receiving some really good feedback on the book, I got on with everyday living.

Thirty five years have passed and my life has changed unbelievably—personally, professionally, and spiritually. Having been pressed to rewrite the book to increase the narrative and to add the changes that have occurred and how we have dealt with them, I have entitled it *My Name Is Ruth 2.0* as homage to the technical world in which we live today. When I use the pronoun "we," I am referring to my family—Charles and our children as well as myself.

Strangely, at least to me, as I reread the book, so many things came into my mind which I wished that I had included: So, I decided to just insert those as well as the chapters at the end to bring this Ruth experience up to date. Therefore, if you were one of those who read the first book, do

not hesitate to read this one from the beginning—
this is not a repeat, this is *My Name Is Ruth 2.0.*

PREFACE

The Beginning

When does a love story begin? Logically, at the beginning, but where is that? At the moment of meeting? With the deepening of relationships? All of this is a part of it. Certainly, a love story begins with ideals instilled and the experiences gained in childhood and adolescence which equip one to love and be loved.

Psychology holds that the qualities for which a girl searches in a husband are those she most admires in her own father, or those she desires him to possess. Therefore, it is not unthinkable to conclude that a love story can begin in childhood. A look backward is a good way to begin this one.

With nostalgia, I think back to my childhood home. Mother, Daddy, my sisters. The things that I thought of as little and insignificant become greatly enhanced—church, Christmas, music, books, trips to visit grandparents, friends, neighbors, Daddy and his basement workshop, the constant reminders to measure up to expectations, schoolwork, and the bickering fun of three younger sisters. There was no time to spend in depression or vacant wanderings. There were chores, school assignments, church participation and Daddy always had a project for us. Mother felt that we should learn how to sew, cook, and kept us busily involved in these activities which included some of the enjoyable things from her own youth as well as modeling what being a wife and mother constituted. Our lives were totally integrated with one another, yet with the urging to be ourselves. Time alone was important then but hard to find and even more difficult to maintain. There were six of us living in a two bedroom house with one bathroom. Think about it: Mother, Daddy and FOUR daughters sharing one bathroom! Today, we cannot conceive of that. But, then, it was normal.

The memory of my father is special to me. The first memories are austere. There was not much money during those post-depression days of my early childhood, yet we had very full lives. My earliest memory is when I was barely two years old. I recall my father holding me on his lap very early in the morning, just at daylight. I had awakened disturbed and crying because I could hear a sound in the next room; and, he had come to comfort me. Having assured me that nothing was wrong and that I should go back to sleep, I heard it again. Holding his ear, I said, "Listen, it's a little chicken!"

Well, turns out, there was no chicken: in the adjacent room, my little sister, Barbara Faye

(Bobbye) was being born! Daddy reassured me and I do not remember anything else until later in the day when I met my sister. She would become not only a sister, but my best friend and confidant. Our relationship would be unique having begun with the tiny sound of "a chicken".

Daddy was instrumental in delivering the news of my next sister some seven years later. Bobbye and I had been taken to our grandparents in the mountains as soon as school was out. Racing to the mail box each morning, we would return with the mail to the breakfast table so that our Granddaddy Sutton could open it and hopefully read it to us. On this morning, he announced that there was a letter from Daddy. Reading it aloud, he told us of the arrival of our new sister, Sherry Diane. Neither of us was too impressed: we had each other which had always been sufficient for us. There were no expectations on our behalf we went on with our vacation. Arriving home later, we accepted her when we met her and decided that she was okay. We would learn very soon that this new sister was beautiful: far more than either of us. Everywhere we went with her, people would share how beautiful she was. We could just see them wondering what had happened to us. But, we learned to live with that and to love her dearly.

Ten years later, I was a high school senior and had been given the responsibility to take care of my sisters while my Daddy took my Mother to the hospital where she would deliver our new sibling. My two sisters and I had spent HOURS praying for a little brother: we were a bit tired of this all girl business. Making an executive decision, I had decreed that we could stay home from school that day to await the news. Sure enough, Daddy telephoned to share the breaking news that we had another little sister, Jill Jeannine. Despite our disappointment at not having a brother, we were thrilled to have a new sibling and could hardly wait to meet her. She would always be the baby of the family and a bane to our existence as sisters.

The four of us began a journey of sisterhood which has involved a lot of give and take, interrupted only when our sister, Bobbye, died shortly before my fortieth birthday. I shall never forget being given that news: she had taken her life. Stunned and reeling, I acknowledged that I had not only lost my sister, but my closest friend, the one who knew me better than anyone. At that time, I had to ask myself how I was going to go on without knowing that she was on the other end of my telephone line whenever I needed her or just wanted to chat. For the three of us who were left, that was the first link in our sisterhood, indeed in our family, to suffer destruction.

Our Father worked very hard at more than one job each day of our young lives to provide for us. He moved from his native mountains to the city to find a job to support us when I was only two.

Even with a college education, finding employment was difficult in those years. When he began to work for the Telephone Company, Bobbye and I thought he was just cool. None of us realized that this was going to be a career that would last for his lifetime and bring him great joy and high rewards. Our Mother also worked very hard to put together a home and sustain it with meals, and a rewarding life. Remembering how hard she had to struggle to make some of these things happen brings tears to my eyes today. The demands on them both were great and made for little opportunity to embrace a child and say, "I love you." We were expected to understand and accept that this went without saying. Our needs, especially the physical ones were met, and we had some of our wants as well. That should have been sufficient in the view of my parents. Most of the time, it was. With adolescence, however, came the stirrings of insecurity born from the sterility of hard working parents and four girls with assorted needs— particularly emotional. The four of us were so different that a blanket act of understanding was impossible. We needed individual attention which was hard to achieve in those days. Yet, this attitude taught us independence and discouraged the "clinging vine" or "apron string" syndrome. We did learn to depend upon one another in many instances. That part of our relationship carries on into our senior adulthood.

A love of knowledge, all knowledge, was imparted to us from the beginning. Books—all books—were highly esteemed. To this day, each of us still treasure books and reads avidly—anything! I had a distinct advantage over my sisters by being the first grandchild on my Father's side. His family descended from a long line of scholars and teachers. So, my memory of sitting on the lap of my Grandfather Sutton is one of my first and best memories. Granddaddy had taught in a one room schoolhouse for years before becoming a college professor. He taught me to read by the time that I was three years old. I entered elementary school ready to conquer the world for I would be able to get my hands on books, books, and more books. None of my sisters had that opportunity for he passed away early in their lives.

In the same vein, my Mother's family had descended from a long line of professionals—doctors, politicians and the like. My Granddaddy Boggs would sit each one of us on his front porch swing and teach us spelling. His favorite activity, even after we were in high school, was for us to spell the alphabet. I still remember how we were amazed that he could spell the letter "H" (aytch). My sister, Bobbye, tried very hard to convince her first grade teacher that was a spelling word.

Naturally coming from that background, we were expected not only to do well in school but to excel. The worst punishment doled out to us was the result of "inadequate" performances in school. Be assured, it was severe and certain. Each of us was expected to perform scholastically to the tune of "A" and perhaps an occasional "B+" but preferably "A+." Extracurricular activities were frowned upon as "frills" and strongly discouraged. So, we came to seek wisdom and always to strive to do our best. This was especially true in Math. Our Father was brilliant in all things related to Math, Geometry, Calculus, Statistics, you name it. Sadly, to say, not a one of us displayed that in our youth, much to his disappointment. While our self-image sometimes suffered trying to meet the expectations, our self-awareness matured quite early.

Understanding was difficult. My parents were uncompromising and even prejudiced in their attitudes. They greatly frowned upon dancing, dating, makeup, and many of the other trappings of youth. A constant battle of wits raged as we tried to convince them, only to be overruled with authority. This made for an unholy allegiance among the four of us—a sort of one for all, all for one confederation not only to convince, but to overcome! It never worked. So, it was that we looked carefully at all activities and friends. This occasioned painstaking judgments and all too often heartbreaking disappointments. Yet, it taught us to share with one another and to take joy from sisterly accomplishments. We learned to trust one another implicitly and to work together for the goals of one another. Jealously was minimal.

Our spiritual lives were cultivated carefully. Daddy was a deacon—in the true sense of the word. Both Mother and Daddy were Sunday school teachers and choir members. Sunday and Wednesday were always reserved for church. We were always at every revival meeting and always went to church while on our vacation. God was an unseen, but acknowledged member of our household. While narrowing activities, we learned a real sense of values by seeing them practiced in the lives of our parents and were led to follow suit in our early youth. We learned to pray early. Ours were not the rote prayers of "Now I lay me down to sleep. . ." or "God is great, God is good." No, we learned to talk to God and to listen to Him as well.

The sibling relationship was valuable. Four girls must share a lot! We shared one bathroom, housework, a bedroom, friends, and more confidences than remembrance can recall. I was really lucky: I got new clothes, they wore hand me downs. We were close in relationships and in goals. We fought with each other and for each other. When united, we were an impenetrable force. Divided, we were a house of cards. We learned to love, hate, give, and take. Our sisterhood is more than a word, it is lives shared.

We continue to share. All of these experiences instilled qualities and expectations in my conscious and subconscious that contributed to the love story that led me to become Ruth.

Growing up, I learned the Biblical story of Ruth and her dedication: "Entreat me not to leave thee, or to return from following after thee: for whither thou goest, I will go; and, where thou lodgest, I will lodge; thy people shall be my people and thy God my God: Where thou diest, will I die, and there will I be buried: the Lord do so to me and more also, if aught but death part thee and me: (Ruth 1:19, 17 KJV). In my teens, I learned to utilize that example in my Christian life and to equate it with being a successful Christian wife and mother. So, my life goals were set with the mainstay being total dedication and the seeking of God's will.

A part of my early training molded my thinking so that I was able to commit myself totally to love. This ability to commit led me to dedicate myself to the God to whom my parents had introduced me early in my life, and to answer His call and so began the love story that today bears repeating.

Knowing that they are not alone is a vital lesson which all young women need to learn. That the experiences which they endure are repeated in the lives of countless others each moment forms a sisterhood that supports the ability to meet the challenge of growing up, finding one's way, and building a life of service and meaning. Yet, so often, we do feel alone. Nothing is more unsettling than being in the midst of the chaos of maturing with the body changes, the thriving hormones, the emotions barely concealed, and feeling totally at sea without a life preserver. Having experienced this for myself and seen it repeated not only in my sisters and my friends but everywhere I turn, I found a mission. Perhaps astrology is right: I am a Leo, the major characteristic of which is leadership. As a very young girl, my Grandfather Sutton saw this in me and told my parents—according to them—"This one is not going to sit still. She is going to set out to change this world. And, she just might do it!" My parents have shared that story with me all of my life. So, I guess, while some call it stubbornness, I felt that God had more in mind for me than sitting idly by being ladylike, and I set out to make a difference very early. Thus, my purpose is to communicate the qualities that Ruth outlined and to which she was committed. In so doing, my name is Ruth.

Chapter One

Discovery

"And the Lord God said, 'It isn't good for man to be alone; I will make a companion for him, a helper suited to his needs' . . . Then the Lord God caused the man to fall into a deep sleep, and took one of his ribs and closed up the place from which he had removed it, and made the rib into a woman, and brought her to the man . . . Adam exclaimed, 'She is part of my own bone and flesh! Her name is 'woman'" . . . This explains why a man leaves his father and mother and is joined to his wife in such a way that the two become one person." (Genesis 2:18, 21 thru 24 TLB) As a teen, this verse grabbed my attention. The creation story alone fascinated me; but, realizing that women were made for such a special mission gave me a feeling of the need to fulfill my mission. That involved growing up and building a home with a partner—falling in love.

Every little girl dreams of the day that her Prince Charming bursts into her life, astride his white charger to sweep her off of her feet, away into a lifetime of love, romance, and "happily ever after." The little girl who grows up to be a Pastor's wife is no different. Love is a strangely wonderful emotion denying all logical explanations. The plainest Jane can be turned into a fairy princess and the most unlikely candidate into Prince Charming. The white charger? Yes, it is also recognizable, but with a bit more imagination . . . perhaps a white Chevrolet with a manual transmission. At least that is what happened in my life.

Growing up at a time when women had not yet gained stature in the church, my Christian ambitions for service were limited because of my gender. I felt that God could use my life as early as adolescence. At the age of fifteen, I began to teach Sunday school in my church never realizing that at age eighty, I would still be doing that. In the Girls Auxiliary missions program of my church, I worked hard on my Forward Steps and achieved the rank of Queen. In those studies, I found out what the Great Commission was all about.

My trip to G.A. Camp Pinnacle where I stayed for a week challenged my Christian testimony and revealed to me that the way of God can not only be found, but can be achieved. In the twilight as we would assemble in the Vesper Garden, I found myself able to communicate with God in a most intimate way, and in the quietness of that place, I learned that He would communicate with me as well. When the women of Georgia Baptist Women's Missionary Union built that camp and included that dedicated place,

The Vesper Garden," they likely had no idea that the hearts and lives of so many girls would be changed forever in that place. Returning from Camp, I knew that my task was to find and follow God's will for my life. That meant making my life mean something.

Enchanted by the stories of people all over the world who had never heard the story of Jesus, I yielded to His will as a sixteen year old dedicating my life to His service, praying for God's direction. Yearning for the "glamor" of the Foreign Mission Field, I dreamed of using my career all over the world. I had wanted to become an architect: that had been my dream for years. But, when God called me to be his witness, that dream did not seem to fit. So, I prayed diligently that God would reveal to me just what I was to do. When I began my college classes, I did not know where my road would lead. In my mission studies, I became acutely aware of the teaching ministry that was the backbone of our mission plan in the Southern Baptist Convention. Everywhere I turned I seemed to see missionaries witnessing and teaching on the mission field. I had always wanted to study English and read all of the wonderful literature and write. In the back of my mind, a new dream began to emerge. I could teach little children how to read and write, telling them of God's love, and of rendering valuable services which I felt incapable of doing. But using my career for God's work, I would be of value to my church. This sounds like a classic story which with proper attention can come true, until that little four letter word comes in—LOVE.

While I was a high school senior, my family moved and we changed churches. That Christmas, a young man spoke to my Sunday School Department in assembly, giving a devotional/testimony. Arriving home that Sunday morning, I told my mother that I had found the man that I would marry. She quickly sized up the magnitude of this momentous decision and replied, "Good. Who is it?" (She was that sort of Mom—unflustered by a daughter's sudden lifetime decision!) For the first time, I realized that I did not know his name. Undaunted, I assured her that I would not only find out his name, but that I would also marry him!

The next week at church, I learned that my dream man had been home on leave from the Air Force for the holidays and had already returned to his base. He would not be coming back for who knew how long. So much for my master plan of allowing him into my dream for the future!

Four months went by and I was asked to help reorganize our Young People's Sunday School Department assisting a young man who would be taking over as Superintendent. While the name did not ring a bell, this was an opportunity to get to work on my dreams. Seizing the opportunity to be of value in God's church, I prayerfully accepted the task. Shortly afterward, I met my associate in this new undertaking—yes, the guy for whom I had fallen at Christmas. Only, this time I learned his name!

We began our task, and I became more aware of Charles as a fellow Christian than a Prince Charming. Obviously, he did not reciprocate my plans and saw me only as a helper in this reorganization plan. Four years older than me, he dated every girl in the church but me! Long before the Women's Liberation movement made it fashionable for girls to invite boys to events, I broke the unwritten law and invited him to my high school graduation ceremony and the party that would follow. We had become very good friends working in the Sunday School Department, so this was not out of the clear blue. Well, not really!

To my eternal consternation, he refused.

Later, I would learn that he said to his friends, "I can't go with her. She is too young!" Yet, he came to my graduation. Amazingly, from the stage of the City Auditorium, as one of two hundred plus graduates, I looked out on the assembled 1,500 plus guests, and saw HIM! My best friend was seated beside me. When I punched her and told her, she too was amazed! He even took me to the party that followed.

As summer wore on, we even, began to date. I suppose this was dating. Primarily we went to Church meetings, Youth for Christ meetings, with an occasional movie or get together with the youth group of our church. Yes, I suppose that is dating. However, interspersed with those "dates" were his real dates with other girls older than me.

Weeks became months and two years went by. We were the best of friends, sharing our hopes, dreams, ambitions, and testimonies. A part of me was still in love, I suppose; but, obviously no part of him looked at me in that way. Our work in our church was going very well. God was using us and we were both happy in the center of His will.

I wish that I could describe sky rockets, or tingles, or something else to convey the depth of emotion I felt during those years, but that was not the case. While I was happy in the center of God's will, there was more, much more to these feelings. I knew that I was in love, and that it was a growing, sharing relationship that could mature into real love. Our relationship was warm and compatible, but certainly not romantic! As I dated other fellows, I found myself to be considered attractive, desirable, and mature. (What an eye opener that was!) With Charles, I was "the kid." He would take me to the movies or for a hamburger and tell me about his dates. Once, he even showed me a ring and asked me if it would make a good engagement ring! That certainly took the wind out of my sails! What changed our relationship defies description—and must be the handiwork of God. That is the only explanation.

Preparing myself to follow my dreams of becoming a missionary, I was going to college at night while working full time as a secretary. With the studying necessary for that and with my church work, and a semblance of a social life, I was very busy. Not so busy, however, to deny that I was in love—even if it was a one way affair. Unable to give up on my dream of the mission field, I was keenly aware that he was very pleased in his job and with his work in the church. Being realistic, those two did not seem to mesh.

Charles began to talk of God leading him into the ministry. Our dates became prayerful, soul searching, meditative encounters. We became an acknowledged "couple." I stopped dating other guys and I believed that he had stopped dating other girls. He began college at night attending classes on different nights than I. Since he had been out of school for four years, he needed help getting back into study habits. I was there to help. A year went by and our lives were going very well. Quarterly finals came along, and he was quite nervous about his English class. He called to say that the exam was over and that he would be by my house to tell me about it. I was sure that he had not done well. When he got there, I was in the kitchen, ironing.

Standing in the door, he asked me, "In the sentence 'He carried the bucket' what is the direct object?" Looking at him, I was distraught. If he had missed that, what must he have done on the rest of the exam? Then, leaning across the ironing board, he placed a diamond ring on the third finger of my left hand and asked me to marry him. Cue in the skyrockets, fireworks, thunder and lightning and all of the rest!

Not very romantic, I know. In fact, in retrospect, it was probably an omen of things to come. Our relationship began with our work in the church, and extended into the rest of our lives together. So, my entrance into the role of a Pastor's wife began over an ironing board; and, I have spent many hours thusly since that time. This is simply "us." The classic fairy tale suffers some when translated into our tale; however, my Prince Charming did come into my life and the "happily ever after" began.

We set our wedding date for twelve weeks later. Our families were shocked. I do not know what his family was thinking, but my parents thought that I was too young—I was nineteen when I became engaged. We forged onward feeling that God was in this. All arrangements were completed and our families became adjusted. The date would be May 2—I had always dreamt of a May wedding in a garden surrounded by spring flowers. The garden was not going to happen, but the spring flowers were ordered and bouquets planned. My dress was purchased and admired almost hourly. The invitations turned out to be so beautiful. Actually, I was so pleased with them that I put one into my Bible and carried it everywhere that I went. This seemed fitting since we had dedicated our relationship to the Lord.

The one thing upon which I had not counted was God being a major player in the planning. Having given my life to God, and with Charles planning our lives together in the center of His will, I was confident. Then, God stepped in and issued the unquestionable "call" to Charles. Accepting the call to full time Christian service meant a new direction—for both of us. With less than a year of college under his belt, Charles had to return to school to obtain a degree before he could even consider going to the Seminary. To accomplish this end and be in the center of God's will required full time attendance in school for him which translated to a totally new concept of our wedding plans. The strangest thing happened. We experienced firsthand what God means when He says, "I want to use you!" People still tell me that they have never heard God, seen Him, or touched Him and therefore cannot believe. Well, I heard Him twice: Once to me at sixteen, and now to both of us. No one can ever tell me that there is no God, I know better.

Without the slightest bit of hysteria, we discussed the matter with the seemingly foregone notion that this was what we were going to do. With only four weeks before our wedding was to take place, we got busy cancelling reservations, returning my wedding dress, destroying the two hundred beautifully engraved invitations, and telling our families. With no reservations on our part, we never anticipated that our parents would be the slightest bit perturbed by this change in plans—but, they were.

My parents felt that I had been "jilted." As they put it, I had been "left at the altar." I had never really gotten to the altar, so that was not accurate; but, they were not pleased. His parents were not all that excited about the fact that he was going to attend college full time in order to enter the ministry. That also bothered my parents. Both of them sat me down and explained that the life I was about to accept would "not be easy." (If there was ever an understatement, this was it!) His parents wondered at his ability to support himself and have a "successful" life as a minister. While we had eagerly embraced this new direction, we met our first stumbling block. Needless to say, this would not be the last. While our mothers commiserated about which one of us had "jilted" the other, our friends clicked in sympathy, sure that our relationship was over.

While we got busy getting Charles accepted into our state's Baptist College, we both continued our jobs full time while continuing our "dating" life. He would be moving into the dorm in September while I continued my job and saved as much money as possible for the wedding that we were now planning seven years hence when he would have his degree and finish Seminary. (Remember, I was only nineteen. Time was nothing to me then!)

What a summer that was! With so much to do to get him ready for school and with our friends and family not understanding at all, we found ourselves in foolish arguments over and over again over absolutely nothing. The pressure was too intense. We traded the diamond ring back and forth several times. My mother became exhausted by my tears and never knowing what was wrong nor understanding why I would not be wearing my ring but still committed to a future with him. His mother tried to mediate all to no avail. Nobody believed that we would ever go through with our declared intentions predicting that he would be back home in no time at all, but that the wedding would never happen. So many times I heard, "Once a wedding is called off, it never happens." That always sounded ridiculous to me! Still does!

Our home church licensed Charles to the gospel ministry. The license document was reluctantly signed by my father—the church clerk. Daddy vowed that we would never see Charles carry through with these stated intentions. (Sixteen years later, he gave Charles a praiseworthy recommendation when a church inquired through a student of his. My mother took longer—twenty six years to be exact!) I am not sure that his family ever really accepted me. There was too much going on with their son to think about it, I suppose. The church family endorsed his call and encouraged him with their good wishes and promises of prayers. The same people looked at me with sympathy in their eyes, and just shook their heads. What a time that was!

Sadly, I bade Charles goodbye as he went off to school—one hundred miles away. We were committed to marrying in seven years. With what I would save from my salary in those years, we would have a start in our new life together when the time came.

It worked too—on paper. Four months later, during Christmas break, we were married.

Ours was a storybook wedding. The bride starry eyed in stunning white satin with happiness glowing in her face met the groom who was tall and handsome wearing a determined look at the altar while both sets of parents were skeptical and the church family was divided as to our future. My sister stood beside me and was totally supportive. Departing the church in the snow to begin a life together, we vowed to give God our best—together!

On that day, Saturday, I privately vowed to God that I would become the helpmate to Charles that God would have me to be. Inside our rings we had engraved the Bible reference, Ruth 1:16, and our soloist sang the hymn containing the words of that verse, "Whither thou goest I will go . . . thy God shall be my God." To me, this said all that needed saying then and now. Together we would become all that God would have us to be. But, the verse meant more than that to me. I felt that it meant that from that day forth, my place would be beside Charles, subject to him, yes; reflecting his commitment and devotion to service as well as fulfilling the commitment I had personally made to God when I was sixteen. We two truly became one.

Yes, I was starry eyed, naïve, and all that goes along with that; but, in my mind, I saw and believed that this was my calling and that I could do it. As my parents had told me, I knew that this would not be the easiest of lives; however, I believed that it would be the way that God was leading. That was sufficient for me.

So it has been—and therein lies the story . . . My Name Is Ruth.

"I charge thee therefore before God, and the Lord Jesus Christ, who shall judge the quick and the dead at his appearing and his kingdom: Preach the word; be instant in season, out of season; reprove, rebuke, exhort with all longsuffering and doctrine."

II Tim. 4:1 thru 2 KJV

DOING HIS WILL
How many times must I hear God call
Before I give Him my all?
And how many times will my selfishness stand
Before I put myself in His hands?
Yes, and how many times must I fail on my own
Before Christ, my Lord, I hail?
The answer my friend, can be found in Him,
Yes, the answer is only found in Him?
How many times will I try on my own,
Before I see I'm alone?
Yes, and how many times will I fall to my knees,
Before I give Him my all?
When will the emptiness inside be filled,
And I begin doing His will?

The answer my friend, can be found in Him,
Yes, the answer is only found in Him.
-        Anonymous

Chapter Two

Accepting the Challenge

God and His works are not easy to explain. One knows what God expects and either does or does not measure up. At the outset, we determined to measure up, to put God first. This was not all that easy, we learned.

After the nine months of tortuous planning and frustration that preceded our marriage, we were at last together and beginning the life to which God had called each of us. All those who had cast doubt on our relationship and subsequent marriage were now far away. We had a brief honeymoon—a time just for us where we recuperated from the stress under which each of us had been laboring for weeks. All too soon, that ended and the first real test of our new relationship came. Charles had agreed to lead the services at our home church for a special Christmas observance. After only four days of marriage, we were back to his parents' home where we shared a bedroom with his teenage brother! All of this was in order to be positioned to follow God leadership. The first step had been taken and our trip into this new life had begun.

School

That New Year's Eve, we spent in our first home: a small apartment in a beautiful, old historic home near the college campus. We finally were able to settle into college life where we quickly learned to live on "poverty row" as married housing at the university was called. One of the facts that made it all bearable was that there were so many others in the same boat with us. In fact, we are lucky—God continued to bless us and I found an excellent job immediately with a great law firm making it possible for Charles to go to school full time. Yet, there was little money, no luxuries, just the peace of knowing that we were where God had placed us, on the way to doing His bidding, and experiencing the joy of at last being together.

My working had to be God's leadership. Within two days of our arriving in the college town, I was given the opportunity to work as a legal secretary in a prominent law firm. While I knew nothing about the legal profession, having only worked in Public Relations and Advertising, I learned quickly. The four partners were all very kind and helpful. One of them was a state politician through whom I met and got to know a number of people who became helpful to us down through the years. Many of my experiences in this job prepared me for the years ahead. The money was good and it made our lives much easier than if Charles had been compelled to take a part time job.

We learned more ways to use hamburger than any Betty Crocker ever imagined. It became our staple! We learned to turn off lights as we left a room, use heat only when necessary, do without air conditioning, and conserve water. Realizing all that our parents had done for us as we grew up was a real awakening. Now we had to do it ourselves. All of this was before the energy crisis too. Utilities were semi luxuries for our shoestrings were short. Yet, we never worried, confident that God would provide.

There was a more valuable lesson in that first home and that first year. We learned real sharing—not just with one another, but with the "real" friends we found. There were many young marrieds like us who had so little money and so much hope but from whom so much was required. There were those more fortunate, or so we thought, whose parents were underwriting their education, or who had been called to full time church Pastorates. In our eyes, they had it made. And, there were those less fortunate than we. Some had sickness, several children, or immediately became pregnant. There were also some who were so homesick that they could not settle into their new lives. Perhaps the saddest were those who could not make the grades and had to leave school to pursue another avenue.

The friends we made, with whom we shared our hamburger and whose spaghetti we shared, found God's will leading them to all four corners of the world. Some went on to Pastorates, some to music ministry positions, some into religious education, and some to the far flung mission fields. The ties of "poverty row" have held us closely in the palm of God's hand.

Just sure that we were so grown up and mature in our planning and living our lives, we were blindsided when on a Sunday night at the evening worship service where Charles was preaching, I stood up with the congregation to join in singing a hymn. As I did, everything went black. A sickening dizzy feeling encompassed my body as I hung onto the back of the pew in front of me to keep from fainting. When some light came into my brain, I sat down puzzled at what had happened and feeling the most terrible pain in my left side. The pain had been aggravating me for a while, but nothing like this. When we were in the car en route home that night, I shared my experience with Charles and we decided that I would see a doctor the next day. That doctor examined me and sent me for an x-ray giving me some pain meds. The x ray was forwarded to a pulmonary specialist whom I saw on the next day. After some extensive testing, we were told that the pain that had gotten my attention was pleurisy. While being treated for the pleurisy, we learned that I had tuberculosis of my left lung.

This was sobering news. Neither of us knew much about TB. The doctor explained the disease to us and how life threatening it could be. He promised us that since we had caught it, there was every reason to believe that I would recover but that this would affect my life. Explaining that the treatments would be on going for some months, I would have to quit my job and remain in bed for these months. Remember, I was the bread winner for us at that time. Further, he said that I would not be able to talk for any period of time again which precluded my teaching Sunday school as I had always done. Additionally, I would not be able to have children nor to experience any type of serious exercise such as cleaning house. As he went on, I felt my future fading away. The only thing that I knew to do was pray—as seriously as I could.

With this prayer in my heart joined by the prayers of Charles, my family and my home church I began my treatments and staying in bed. I could not bear being bedridden. My father acquired a television set for me so that I would have some type of distraction during the long hours. That was new for a bit but got old fast.

The law firm where I had worked gave me my typewriter when I resigned. Their promise was that when I was able, they would "keep me busy." Praise God!

I immediately saw that staying in bed was not good for me. Together with God, I devised a plan where I could work for a while, sitting up straight with no slouching to give my lung full extension, then to rest when I felt the fatigue or pain coming along. With a supply of library books and some work from the firm, I set up a little work area by the windows and within two weeks was working about fifteen hours a week. When I saw the doctor, I did not tell him that I was doing this. He examined me and was happy with my condition. So, I kept it up.

My neighbor who had become a good friend knew that I sewed all of my clothes and asked if I would make her daughter's prom dress. She was willing to pay me handsomely. So, I did. Substituting my sewing machine for the typewriter, I made that dress which pleased her so much that I made several shirts and dresses for her daughter and for her. This supplemented my income and helped us so much.

Then, we had the bright idea that since the college Charles was attending had a law school and I was familiar with typing legal papers, especially briefs, there was a venue for more income. So, he posted a notice on their bulletin that I would type for one dollar a page. The response was terrific. Soon I was working twenty five hours a week. Still no problem with the doctor. So, I kept on working until I was tired, then resting, taking my meds, and eating right.

Before too many weeks went by, I was doing the housekeeping and cooking and up to forty hours a week, because I could work at night while Charles studied and on the weekends. We agreed that I would not tell the doctor but that if he saw any problems I would back off. He NEVER saw a problem. I made terrific progress. Charles began to give me my shots at home so that saved me a lot of time and energy.

When I felt like it, I would go with Charles on Sundays. My prayers continued as fervent as ever if not more so. I was determined in my heart to be well and back to myself. Before a year was out, I took a temporary job working forty hours a week and cut back on my work at home. Before that job ended, it was time for Charles to graduate. We had made it despite the curve we had been thrown.

To this day, I have pain in my left lung which has given me pulmonary problems complicated by my childhood asthma. I not only went back to teaching Sunday school, I taught school full time. True, I never had biological children, but I reared three. I have always done my own housework and my own yard work which included mowing, gardening, building a wall when I was seventy five years old, and am still standing. Pneumonia is my worst enemy along with smoke and cold, cold air. I try to keep myself as healthy as possible. I still cannot even consider staying in bed all of the time. Oh, I can sleep an hour or two after the alarm goes off, but no such thing as full time in bed!

Do you see how God blessed us? In our darkest hours when we thought that our goals and dreams were out of the question, when doctors and my family thought that it was all over for us, the light shone through and God just worked His way and all things worked together for His good.

School was hard for Charles. Having been out of school for so long, taking notes and studying as well as writing papers dismayed him. Having gone directly from high school into college at night, I was still in the mode of school, so I could help him. There were many long nights and frustrations, but within three years he graduated.

Learning

There were many supply preaching opportunities in small churches throughout Southern and

Middle Georgia while he was in school. These opportunities made for GREAT experience for his future and also a bit of extra money. There had to be a beginning. I shall never forget the first sermon Charles delivered. He labored long in preparation, making extensive notes which he then condensed and further condensed the condensation. Finally, the day dawned—the weather was hot and humid. There is no place that will compare to Southeast Georgia in the midsummer. The drive through the early Sunday morning would have been exhilarating had we not been so totally terrified!

Finally, we arrived at the small rural church. Picturesque in its setting of tall green pine trees and a carpet of white sand, it rose in its white clapboard majesty to claim the blue of God's sky. The weather was so hot that the windows had to remain open allowing all the gnats in the area to come into the sanctuary. There were many times more gnats than congregation! The song service went well. The prayers were meaningful and the offering was taken. As the time for the message grew closer, I got more and more nervous. When Charles stood to deliver his very first sermon, I knew what "Pray without ceasing" really meant. I was doing it! After an eternity passed, the message ended and the invitation hymn was announced. I was astonished to find that only twelve minutes had passed! Little did I know that there would be many times in the future when I wished that his sermons were that brief! At last, the first REAL step was taken to begin Charles's total response to God's call to the gospel ministry.

There were many other such Sundays as Charles filled pulpits as a supply minister in rural churches, town churches, and city churches all over Georgia. He got so much better at preparing and I gradually got better at sitting in the pew. But, that first Sunday, we both learned more than in all the years of school. We began learning people.

Both of us had come from families who lived in the city, fathers who worked, mothers who were full time homemakers, and a church where everything just seemed to go off like clockwork with no effort from anyone. We had some idea of what the Pastor did but the ministering to the people in their setting was far from both of us.

We learned how to graciously enter homes where we were invited: to accept the hospitality of perfect strangers, to rely totally on God for strength, and for wisdom believing that He would answer. In farming communities we learned how to commiserate over the lack of rain or the price of crops. We met farmers who totally relied on the promises of God to bring the rain when needed. Of great value was listening to these farmers explain how they decided WHAT to plant WHERE and how to go about harvesting and selling. I never enter a super market even now without understanding what some farmers have done to bring these goods to that store. Town churches gave us a glimpse of people who were totally dependent upon their neighbors for any economic success. There were doctors who had come from faraway places to practice medicine in these small towns. Attorneys who had gone away to school and come back home to practice had a great deal to teach us. Storekeepers who had grown up in the town and followed their fathers' footsteps into business amazed us. Yes, we learned people.

From all of these people in places large and small we met people who relied totally on God for their daily living. Some of these people were financially comfortable, even successful, and some, like us, were laboring to stretch their dollars. But, the connection between all of them with their families and fellow church members convinced us anew that when God's will is followed and His work advanced, He gives strength, courage, and the ability to meet each day with a smile. We asked God to supply that for us

And, He did!

On every trip as a pulpit supply, I was mortified thinking that people would be expecting an older woman with her hair in a bun, able to play the piano, and with all of the answers. Talk about stereotypes! I was twenty years old, unable to do anything and had all of the questions with no answers. Each preaching opportunity gave us exposure to different types of people in different areas with somewhat different expectations. One of my greatest attributes at that time was that I was more willing to listen than to speak. I garnered recipes for so many delicious foods with detailed instructions on how to prepare them. The women in the churches were thrilled when I would ask about their masterpieces and would go to great details. To this day, I treasure those times and those recipes which have stood the test of time. Often, I would feel so inadequate. There was really nothing that I could do except be there. After all, I remembered that I had signed on to be the helpmeet and remembered Ruth's words: "Whither thou goest…" These times were learning times for me . . . valuable learning times. I am confident that not a one of those kind people remember me: but, I remember every one of them. Whenever I have called up some of these experiences to help me through a trying time, I thank God for each of them. I vowed to always help some other young woman who was trying to be a Ruth.

The willingness of most of these people to accept me as a young woman—almost a girl—and to feel benevolent toward me still amazes me. Still, I longed for help. If only I had a book to read on

"How to Be a Preacher's Wife," or "1500 Things to Do When You Are the Visiting Preacher's Wife." The kindly counsel of an experienced woman would have been so beneficial. Instead, all I had were brief "sharing times" with other "poverty row" wives, who like me, were not likely to divulge mistakes only victories. We quickly learned the importance of putting the entire situation in the hands of God and thereby locating strength to withstand, and most important, to measure up!

During the last year of college, a small church where Charles had supplied called him back to supply again. After a few Sundays of just filling in, they issued him a Call and he had his first Pastorate. This moved us to another level of experience with the need to be an administrator and work with people in depth. For me, this became a much deeper experience as I became an Adult Sunday School Teacher and worked with the youth. Now, remember with all of this added responsibility, Charles was still in school carrying a full load of subjects and I was working full time. Add to this that we were driving back and forth over a hundred miles one way to our church. Yet, there was such a thrill in driving up to that building every Sunday morning that we never considered the cost. The fatigue of the week just went away and a new day dawned for us. Of course, Monday mornings were difficult since we never got home on Sunday night until around midnight. But, God gave us the strength.

Many of these same experiences followed me to the Seminary where I went through the "student preacher's wife" bit again. "Poverty row" was not so real for us at the Seminary in New Orleans. God, in His infinite wisdom led me to a very good job with the U.S. Army. Again, I had a great job within four days of moving to New Orleans. My working resume became more interesting as I had moved from the high school jobs of clerking in a dime store, to summer jobs typing, to full time work in Public Relations and Advertising, to legal secretary, to secretary to a corporate vice president and now as a secretary to a Captain and liaison for our location. We lived a lot better as a result thereof. By now, we were living much closer to God, as well, which made all things more bearable.

Seminary years were happy ones. Campus life was totally different from college. There was a unity for all of the students were preparing to serve God full time somewhere in some capacity. Again, there were lifelong friendships established that have spanned time and the globe as some have become ". . . witnesses to the uttermost parts of the world," while we have remained ". . . in Jerusalem." Because we did not live on campus (we were not eligible since we had no children), we made many friends among the New

Orleans folks in our apartment complex and, of course, in my office. Many of these people were in utter amazement to learn that we had left Georgia to come to Louisiana under the leadership of God. They loved sharing our experiences as Charles again filled pulpits as a supply all over Southern Louisiana and Western Mississippi. From our off campus friends we learned many of the folkways and mores of the Cajun people that served us well as we went into the churches in the unfamiliar swamps of Southern Louisiana. We learned about eating foods of which we had never heard and meeting people who came to church in dugout canoes. Yes, Seminary life was much different than our college life had been.

By now, being a "preacher's wife" was a badge that I had learned to wear with humble pride. I was quickly accepted by my Roman Catholic coworkers who went to great lengths not to curse in front of me. Arriving in the Motor Pool one morning to make a surprise inspection, I had to bow my head to hide my grin when the Supervisor yelled to all of the employees, "Watch your language, Pat is here!"

Under God's leadership, I found a way to put a New Testament with the marked plan of salvation into the hands of a young Catholic man who was so impressed that he shared it with all of the members of that Motor Pool. When he returned the Testament, it was dog eared and greasy. Wearing a big smile, he told me what I wanted to know, yet found unbelievable. He found the courage to say the words, "We'd like you to tell us about this." I did! I almost preached! My young friend was equally amazed when I assured him that the little Testament was his to keep. Eventually, I found testaments for all of them and for others throughout our installation as the word spread about Jesus. When one of the officers called me into his office with a testament in his hand, I was terrified. He asked me, "Do you know this Jesus? Are you saved? Is this why you smile?" My affirmative answer came from a rejoicing soul. I lived each moment in a special place, the center of God's will, a place that my coworkers had not yet found. In my heart, I vowed to try to make my life a better example, and to attempt to better lead others. What a joy it was to grow spiritually, gaining the courage to say what I felt, letting my friends know that I was praying for them and with them. Our Commander accused me of turning the depot into a "revival meeting," but as he said it, he smiled.

So it was that I learned the true value of a day to day Christian witness without words and that the value of a smile conveys Christian living as well as simple friendship and has merit in more ways than I ever dreamed. Needless to say, the entire staff was not won, but I felt that I had come a long way toward understanding how to adapt to a culture without sacrificing ANY of my convictions and beliefs.

Almost three years had passed and I was growing more and more comfortable with my role and the lessons I was being taught on a daily basis as my conviction to live a God centered life really took roots. Then, Charles had finished his studies at Seminary and it was time for us to move on to the next step of our lives. Accepting a full time Pastorate in a small Georgia town, we were called to move again. I turned in my resignation and the girls gave me a "going away party" at an exclusive French Quarter restaurant. I was so impressed! A real joy came when on my last morning I came to my desk to find it piled with little gifts from the men—inspectors, motor pool mechanics, the top civilian supervisors and the Army Brass. The experience was almost like hearing a "Well done, thou good and faithful servant" (Matthew 25:23). As I left with Charles, we embarked on a new episode of our lives as we walked the path God spread before us.

Many years have passed, and in government reorganization the depot where I worked has been absorbed into another Command and become a part of NASA. For years, I still heard from those with whom I worked in New Orleans, and from whom I learned the value of just being me. A Baptist among the Catholics does not have to be oil with water. God really does "work in mysterious ways His wonders to perform" as William Cowper wrote in the nineteenth century.

Ordination

The various churches to which Charles was led have ranged from the rural church to the small village church to a mission church to a city church. Each Pastorate is distinctive. Each is special. Each has its high points and its low points. Looking back, I thank God for leading Charles and me to each one of them.

The very first opportunity that came to Charles was a tiny church in a very small railroad community in East Georgia. Here we were "so young." At the request of this church, Charles was ordained to the gospel ministry—truly set aside. We had been married for two years and the "romance" of the ministry was still there. I was twenty one, he was twenty five. He was still a student in college when this opportunity was presented. Ordination is the privilege of the home church to conduct an inquiry into the candidate's background, commitment, education, and calling. This procedure surpasses the background check and looks into the heart, mind, and soul of the candidate. Heretofore, he had been a licensed minister but not able to fulfill all of the duties of a Pastor—baptism, marriage, the

Lord's Supper, and dealing with finances and administration. When the church called Charles, they knew that he would have to be ordained and sent that request to our home church. The men who sat on the Ordination Committee included our Pastor, a representative from the calling church, the former Pastor who had led Charles to Christ, the former Pastor of mine who had baptized me, and a representative of the State Convention.

Following the Committee meeting, a date was set for the Ordination Ceremony which was held at our home church with the Pastors from the Committee present to give reports. Totally unprepared for the formality of the occasion, I was surprised to see almost all of our old friends present, along with all of the girls who had been in the youth group I had led and the young people from the Sunday School class that I had taught. We had invited our immediate families of course, and they invited our extended families who responded to the seriousness of our life commitment and were present. Our Pastor who had performed our marriage ceremony preached the Ordination Sermon. He said, "Charles, now that you have made this step, there is no turning back." Hearing those words, I realized anew the depth of the "call" he had experienced; but, I could not realize the heartache, loneliness, supreme joy or fulfillment that would accompany that fact. Knowing that we were doing God's will, there was a confidence born in that hour that would be called upon many times in the ensuing years.

As the laying on of hands was concluded, our Pastor called me to join Charles at the front. He said, "You will stand by him for all of the years ahead, so it is only right that you begin now." I stood proudly beside Charles to greet the people of our home church who assured us of their love and prayers. Our family members embraced us and shared their love and continued prayers for us. Indeed, it was a high pinnacle of spiritual experience. We were lifted to a plateau on which we had never before stood. Little did we know the awe with which we should have faced the future. I suppose God chooses to light the way only dimly, otherwise, we might turn back quickly out of fear and loss of confidence. On that day, the light, no matter how dim, was more than enough.

Through the years, many of my Pastor's wife friends have lamented their lot in life. Some bemoan the lack of money and the need for things, others despair about the lack of time together, the frequent middle of the night calls, the demands made upon their husbands' time, not being able to build a dream house, homesickness, and a litany of other complaints. This, I learned at last was common and not always warnings of failure. But, there was one of our Seminary friends who called me one day, weeping loudly and saying, "I was not CALLED, I was ASKED!" Her disappointments were so severe that they were unable to overcome them and a divorce brought her Ruth experience to an abrupt halt!

Another time, a Pastor's wife friend called me weeping. We lived about fifty miles apart at that time, so a meeting was difficult. Instead, we talked by phone. Her voice ragged with pain, she told me that her husband had been discovered by some of the deacons of his church to be having affair with a very young woman. Shocked! I continued to listen with disbelief. She told me of the evidence that they had presented of his meetings with this woman, the gifts he had purchased for her, and the trip they had taken together when she thought that he was at a denominational meeting. With her two children, she was preparing to leave and return to her parents' home in another state. She was humiliated. My task was to listen to her and to pray with her. I had no advice. This was so far beyond my understanding that I was aching with pain trying to comprehend and help my friend who was so desperate. She did leave with her children never to return. He left the ministry in disgrace. We never knew what happened to him eventually, but she stayed in her home town eventually getting a job as a church Minister of Music and rearing her children alone.

There are all kinds of ministers/preachers. There are all kinds of wives. The title that goes with being a minister's wife is distinctive and requires the surrender of some of life's experiences. When trying to fulfill the role in the way that Ruth laid it out, one has to give up all to the role that God chooses to be played. When that plan is disrupted by Satan, and it is disrupted as are the lives of all Christians from time to time, the price is very high. Only God in His infinite mercy can understand and comfort.

Other of my Pastors' wife friends have shouted their joy at God's plan for them. Ordination engraved indelibly on my heart and soul our unique "specialness." The wives often shared phone calls after a particularly rewarding Sunday service or experience. From one another we drew strength to do the task God had set before us. While we were spread across the miles, there was always the sisterhood that drew us close. Many years later, I was honored to serve as an officer of our State Convention's Pastor's Wives Conference where I saw repeated manifold the outstanding friendships and dedication that a Ruth gives to her husband and his ministry. In fact, I can honestly say that there are many churches who appreciate their Pastor's wife as much as their Pastor! Those are the churches that get "two for the price of one." No Pastor's wife receives a salary or recognition, but her task is there to be completed in the way that God leads her.

My personal experience with the Son of God had led me to full surrender five years before that Ordination day. At that time, I had envisioned myself a maiden missionary in Africa giving my all for God. There has been no less excitement or diversification in being a dedicated Pastor's wife giving my all for God beside my husband right here in my native land. Indeed, even in July in South Georgia without air conditioning I sometimes wonder if I have not been transported to that tropical place!

You see, I love my "lot" in life. A friend confided she would not get involved in her husband's ministry. She intimated that she felt no need to be a part of it herself. I feel great sadness for her and the many others who may share her emotions. Perhaps there is truth that the wife of an accountant, an attorney, a plumber, or an insurance salesman feels no need to learn that occupation or to be involved directly in it. I wish that they could all experience the sheer joy of being called by God to be a Ruth. Total surrender brings boundless joy.

Truly, I believe that our marriage was strengthened by our dedication to the ministry together. I know that as we worked toward common goals we certainly have learned from one another how to be better Christians and, in turn, better mate. At times, we even act as one person as we make decisions and interact with others.

"Preach the word; be instant in season, out of season; reprove, rebuke, exhort with all longsuffering and doctrine."
-       II Timothy 4:2 KJV

My Pastor

I like the word "Pastor." It makes me think of Jesus the Shepherd. I like my Pastor, the under shepherd. I like the way he smiles and jokes and shakes hands. But people who know say a Pastor is a lonely man, for he has no Pastor, no human being to whom he can go and receive help and comfort and strength. My Pastor has no earthly shepherd. I think our Pastor is the best, because he belongs to me. His ministry is partly mine because I pray for him. He is a good preacher, not because he figured out how to be one all by himself, but because he prays and because I pray for him; and God answers prayers like that. I thank God for my Pastor.

Patricia Sutton

1949

Chapter Three

Getting Down to Business

With preparations underway to go about the business of Pastoring, and with the assurance of commitment, the time had come to "get down to business." Somehow, we had to determine if we could really spend our lives in service, or if this was just one of those dreams that are impossible to achieve. With our lives and ministry in God's hands, we became true instruments for His service.

Camak Baptist Church

Among the churches where Charles had served as a supply minister there was one that became very important to us. He supply preached there three times over a period of about a year. Several months passed, and he got a request to preach again at which time the Pulpit Committee talked to him about becoming their Pastor and called for his Ordination. A very small town adjacent to a rock quarry and a railroad community, Camak provided us with our very first Pastorate.
Since Charles was still in school, we commuted back and forth on Sundays for a few months during which time Charles finished school, graduated, and we prepared ourselves to move

onto the church field. This was a very "grown up" thing to be doing, and also a very big step forward into what God had called us. This was also a huge leap of faith. We had been living in a small apartment for our entire marriage with super markets and all of the conveniences right at our finger tips. Now, we would be moving into a house which the church was renting for us, where we would have the opportunity to fill up rooms and have a "real life" and nothing was nearby except the railroad depot and a tiny gas station. We would also have to be responsible for all of the things that until now, our landlord had done for us.

The church was quite beautiful: an old building built of locally made dark bricks with a beautiful arched stained glass window. Sitting in a grove of pine trees, the parking lot was out front and entirely sand. This was Eastern Georgia. The sanctuary was in front with a small choir loft to the right which is where the organ sat. The organ was interesting, very old and powered by a Hoover vacuum cleaner.

The most exciting part of these preparations was the knowledge that God was calling Charles to this place, this church, these people and would use Him to glorify His kingdom by winning souls and enriching the saved. While he had been preaching now for a while, he had never had to administer a program, baptize, nor administer the

Lord's Supper. He was going to be a Pastor! Now, that was a "grown up" realization.

After college graduation, we moved from the college town onto the church field about a hundred miles away, still a hundred miles from our families. Now, this was our first move as a married couple and it was hilarious. This was a tiny little church in a very small town. They had no Pastor's home but had rented a home for us— a very large, old clapboard house with huge rooms and a large front porch. The kitchen was at the back of the house and almost as big as our entire apartment. The bathroom had been added years after the house was built and took up part of what would have been the hall down the middle of the house: so the bathroom was immediately in front of the front door of the house. Sitting twelve steps off of the ground, on a huge corner lot, we felt this was our castle. The front yard was all sand. We never had to mow, just rake.

We had been living in nice little one bedroom apartment with bedroom furniture from my parents' home, new living room furniture that we bought with our savings, a used refrigerator, our clothes, and books. Of course there were also the wedding gifts—china, silver, fabulous things that we could not use in that small apartment but which we now knew that we could bring out and enjoy. Moving into that house was such a joyous experience. We had gotten a breakfast room set from under the house of a relative, a mobile washing machine from his sister, and a few other used items from our families. Where I may have dreamed of this well-appointed home with all of the comforts I had enjoyed growing up, I came into a bare house with our meager belongings and thought that I was in heaven! I shall never forget that joy. I recall awaking on the first morning and thinking, "This is our house—OUR HOUSE!" And, then thanking God for bringing us here.

We were somewhat of a novelty in the community. We had no children, we came from the "city," we were starry eyed with big plans, and the assurance that they could not be undone. The Pastor before us had been the father of five children, married for years, with a plethora of household goods—most were antiques. We were "children" in the eyes of the community, but we were determined. What a high this was! There would be other Pastor's homes—some smaller, some larger, some worse, some better—but this was the first one. I smile just thinking back to those moments. Ruth likely would have had similar feelings had she been going into a home—she was a migrant and not afforded this luxury. Her faith, I know, would not have faltered, and I refused to let mine even quiver.

Of course, there were big responsibilities to assume. I would not be needed to type up legal briefs or hurry to the courthouse to file a paper. Instead, I became a teacher for an adult ladies' Sunday school class. All of the members of the class were older than my mother. (At that time she was about forty three and I thought that was so very old!) Further, I found myself a member of two Missionary groups—a day and a night group. Moreover, I was leader for a group of young girls in Girls' Auxiliary. As a young girl, I had found my niche in God's service as a member of Girls' Auxiliary. My commitment had been reinforced when I went to our state G.A. Camp Pinnacle and even more so when I returned there each year as a counselor. So I was thrilled to undertake this responsibility. Our work went well. We loved the people and they seemed to love us. Our home was always open and we enjoyed the young people and the adults. The Pastor's home was ancient with ceilings so high that we could have played basketball inside! With our meager "early matrimony" furniture, we set up housekeeping and nobody thought less of us. The confidence of being young, happy and in the center of God's will still warms my heart to this day despite the years that have passed.

That first winter, we both had the Asian flu at the same time. We were so sick that we were in bed in different rooms, taking turns getting up for medicine and water. Truly, I believe that we were trying to die: the experience was so horrible. The church family had learned of our sickness and knowing of Charles's fondness for sweet potatoes and turnip greens began bringing us food. You guessed it! We had so many sweet potato and turnip green dishes even the dog quit eating it! But, we survived and to this day still love that food combination. God does provide!

A very special memory is of Charles and his first Baptism service. One of the things that the Seminary had NOT prepared him to do was to perform a baptism. In the Baptist church, when one makes a profession of faith in the Lord Jesus Christ, (s)he is baptized which takes place in the church baptistery and involves the "dipping or dunking" of the candidate, symbolizing the dying to sin and resurrection to a new life—following the example of Jesus Christ who was baptized at the outset of His earthly ministry in the Sea of Galilee by John the Baptist. Baptist churches are constructed with a baptism pool behind the podium/choir loft. Long ago, baptizing was done in a nearby lake, river, or creek. Now the pools are built at the time of construction and provide for heated water.

Camak had a baptistery but the water was not heated and came from a nearby spring—a wee bit icy, shall we say? Since Charles had never performed a baptism and there were candidates waiting, the baptism service was scheduled. On that Sunday afternoon, aware that the pool had been filled and deciding that he must practice, I was tapped to participate in this session. I donned my bathing suit; and, we went to the church where Charles baptized me over and over until he was secure enough to perform the real thing that night. While I remember it as an opportunity for us to help one another, I have often felt that I was drawn closer to my Lord God that day as I was repeatedly "baptized." That has helped me enormously by reinforcing my precious relationship with my Savior. To this day, a baptism service in my church affects me for I remember that day and what it meant to my Christian life.

There were so many wonderful experiences there. We were so young and eager that we anxiously sought them out. One of our first new experiences was holding a Vacation Bible School. Because the community was small and the Methodist church was not holding one, our church decided to make this a community wide Bible School. Since neither the Methodist church nor our church was large enough to accommodate so many children, we decided to use the abandoned elementary school building which existed in the community. Since it had not been used in many years, we had a community cleaning of the facility. People came from throughout the environs and cleaned the classrooms and the auditorium. By time for our

Bible School, the building was "spic and span."
At the end of our week of Bible School, we had
commencement for which we practiced that
morning. I was directing the service on the stage
of the auditorium and as I backed up to get a look
at the layout, I stepped off of the stage backward
and hit the concrete floor. I was not injured
badly, unless you want to count my pride. Here I
was trying so hard to be mature and do the right
thing, and there I was sprawled on the floor with
a badly sprained ankle! I was so embarrassed.
Until this day, I can feel the heat rising in my
face! But, that night we had the Commencement
and the Bible School was declared a success with
seventeen professions of faith from our church
alone.

Charles and I had wanted children and in this the
third year of our marriage that had not happened.
So, we got a dog. Butch was a solid black
Labrador retriever. This dog was so smart and
we loved him so much. He learned to ride in the
car with Charles as he visited members and
attended to his duties in the church. Butch would
lie beneath Charles's desk while he studied the
epitome of man's best friend. I think that we
treated him like the child we did not have. After
not quite a year, Butch came up missing. We
searched and searched for him. The people in the
community knew of our dog and our love for him
and joined us in our search. We could not find
him! We were both so sad. We realized how we

had made him a member of our family. After a week of searching, we learned that one of the neighbors, just across the road, had shot him as a reaction to Charles's sermon on tithing. Remember now, I was very young, so I decided to talk to the man's wife, who ordered me off of their property and told me that we got what we deserved. My heart was broken. I wept and was inconsolable. This was such a sobering moment for me. I learned some great lessons: all people are not kind (I had been reared to believe that they were), tithing is a "hot button issue," and to keep my mouth shut and allow the good Lord to handle folks!

A neighbor called to tell us that her dog had puppies and we were welcome to come and select one for ourselves. Confident that no dog could ever replace Butch, I allowed her to talk me into a new dog. Charles and I walked to their house and stood watching the puppies and their mother. They were adorable—little terrier mixes. I fell in love with a little brown and white one who seemed quite lively and came to me willingly. We took her home and named her Friskie: she lived with us for the next sixteen years.

After some time in this first church, Charles began to feel that God was leading him to further his education at a seminary. For us, this was indeed a big decision. We had found a home, security, a life, and a future. The church was small enough for us to be able to adequately minister and learn. Each experience was new and maturing. Seemingly, we had come to the exact spot God wanted—for this brief time. We prayed long and hard about the decision. Because of our common love for the mission field, we looked into the Baptist Seminary in New Orleans. The tuition in seminaries is a gift from Southern Baptists, but living expenses are the responsibility of the student. Plus, we would have to move across the country. So, we needed money.

God provides!

In the town a few miles away there was a large national corporation that manufactured mobile homes. Fortuitously, there was a vacancy for a private secretary's position working for the vice president. This was a marvelous opportunity and my experience qualified me for it. The job was interesting, the salary fantastic, and the hours convenient. One problem arose: we had only one car. I would need to drive the distance to and from work and Charles would need the car to do the work of visiting hospitals and homes. So, with our meager savings, we bought a used car— an old black four door Ford. This took a real leap of faith. We needed money for the move yet we were spending all that we had. This was considered "spending money to make money," at least in our eyes. Much prayer went into this decision. God provided for us.

I had my OWN car. When my father taught me to drive, he declared that my driving was going to cause him to lose his religion. Now, I had my own car and would be driving EVERY day. I was unbelievably happy. Working there for over two years, I was able to save enough money to get us to New Orleans, rent an apartment, live for a while, and set up in a new life there with a nest egg in case of emergencies. For the entire time that I worked there, I knew that God was making a way for Charles to attend the seminary. This was a great time for me. I learned to multi task by working full time and still keeping all of my obligations at home and my opportunities in the church going full time as well.

Every penny possible was saved, applications were made, references gathered, and prayers ascended that God would lead us in this decision of choosing a seminary. Out of the five choices within the Southern Baptist Convention: Louisville, Kentucky, offered its established reputation and seemingly majored on teaching; Southeastern at Wake Forest, North Carolina, was closer to home and, at that time, brand new; Southwestern at Fort Worth, Texas, seemed to be the premier seminary emphasizing the Bible; Golden Gate at Mill Valley, California, was also new and in a "pioneer" area, a tourist attraction for us; and, New Orleans at New Orleans, Louisiana, established and with a missions emphasis.

How the choice was made is still not really clear. In the decision to attend Seminary, we had depended on God to reveal the way. He just seemed to point continually to New Orleans and the pieces fell into place for Charles to enter there. The years have proven this to be an extremely wise choice. The missions emphasis helped us to establish firmly grounded, well informed missionary organizations that have touched many lives and to lead churches to make worthwhile gifts to missions. The association with mission volunteers has given us friends around the world, and brought them to our church homes as they furloughed. Moreover, it has stimulated us to follow with our own lives the challenge of Matthew 28:19 thru 20, "Go ye therefore, and teach all nations, baptizing them in the name of the Father, and of the Son and of the Holy Ghost: Teaching them to observe all things whatsoever I have commanded you; and, lo, I am with you always, even unto the end of the world." While Seminary friends fanned out across the globe, my bout with tuberculosis insured that our mission would be at home. While that was disappointing to me, I was firmly shown that this was where I needed to be, when one of my G.A. girls surrendered her life to be a teaching missionary. As the years rolled along, she completed her studies and preparation, and sure enough, she was sent to Nigeria where she served for seventeen years. My teenage mission dream came true, just with a twist.

We lived in Camak for almost three years before leaving to attend Seminary. One of the most difficult tasks ever faced is the one to leave a church field where there has been so much happiness and growth. Saying farewell to my job was a bit sad, but saying goodbye to the ladies who had taught me more about cooking than I had ever dreamed possible, to the girls in my auxiliary group, the women in my Sunday school class, and the church body as a whole was one of the most emotionally draining experiences of my life. I was not prepared for the closeness that had developed and which would be repeated other times in my life.

The Seminary

On the terrazzo floor of the Dining Hall of New Orleans Baptist Theological Seminary is a large representation of the seal of the school with these words: "Go ye therefore . . . and make disciples." (Matthew 28:19 thru 20 KJV). The echo of this thrilling challenge echoes within the souls of all who enter there. I know that on our first day in that building we were struck with those words and what they said to us about our lives. This was a time of rededication of our lives to God's service whenever and wherever.

While in college, our friends had been from a number of disciplines, but here in New Orleans, our school friends were dedicated to the service of God just as we were. There was something so special about sharing that commitment with so many just like us, and regularly sitting at the feet of the men and women who had served, were serving, and now teaching others to "Go, ye. .". With these people we shared our groceries, our home, our dreams, and our prayers. The community was so close knit that we shared everything. Still with no children of our own, we would often babysit for friends who were off to a church to supply on a Sunday. At times, we would watch the children of some of our friends who needed a night away, or study time. Often the wives would get together for lunch on a Saturday where we would share experiences and offer advice and help if needed. The overall climate at New Orleans Seminary was one of sharing and learning all of the time. There seemed to be something to learn wherever we turned.

The ability to be with these wives was special for me. For the first time, I was able to glean wisdom from women who had given up their personal dreams to follow their husbands into this place of preparation. Few of these women were my age, some were a little older, and some were a good bit older. One woman to whom I was especially drawn had five children and was a college graduate. She and her husband had joint careers and were successful in the corporate world. They had owned a beautiful home near their parents when they answered God's call. In that home each of the children had their own bedroom along with a large backyard and a pool. At the Seminary they lived in a two bedroom apartment with no yard at all, just a playground down the way which they shared with all of the other Seminary children. There was childcare available at the Seminary for the children while this wife worked an entry level clerical job. Whenever I would get discouraged, I would think of this woman and all that she had left behind to follow her husband. I held her up as the ideal representation of Ruth of the Bible.

Valuing my friendship with some of these wives, I decided that there needed to be a way to incorporate all of the wives into some sort of sharing opportunity. After all, we were all seeking the same thing in our lives—to be the support that our husbands needed. We were from all over the country, all ages, some with and some without children, but all with something to offer the others. Given an opportunity to speak with the wife of the President of the Seminary (which I shall never forget and at which I was scared to death), I shared my vision along with the awareness of what such an organization could mean. Using her influence, she opened her home and invited all of the wives to a reception there. Her home was so beautiful—filled with reminders of the decades of service she and her husband had given to the mission fields. Getting to visit inside was such a thrill that the turnout was very good. In that moment was born a new circle of friends that has lasted the decades since its inception and spanned the globe many times over. We decided that we would be a part of Women's Missionary Union of the Southern Baptist Convention and use our gatherings to learn as well as to fellowship. This organization proved to be an effective tool for my life from then onward. The second meeting was held in our apartment—a far cry from the beautiful home of the President of the Seminary, but still, it was what we all knew and lived with daily. Smiles still broaden my face remembering that night and the beautiful women who were in my living room. God truly blessed us. I was never happier.

During our seminary days, there were more supply preaching "assignments." They ranged in Louisiana, Mississippi, and Alabama. These were considered opportunities, and all too rare. After all, every student in the seminary was available to fill a pulpit on very short notice. Not only were they eagerly sought for the money— paying from $5 to $50 per Sunday—but for the experience. All of the students needed money and the poise that could be gained. The exposure was of infinite value. There was always the possibility that a simple supply opportunity might lead to a pulpit recommendation. That had already happened to us once and had been very positive.

One such opportunity came to us in Alabama. This required a 150 mile trip one way from our home in New Orleans. With our faithful dog, we set out. This was a rural church. (We had learned early in our college supply days, never to say "country church.") The people were warm and supportive as well as responsive so it was a thoroughly inspiring day. After the Evening Service, the time that the honorarium is usually given, Charles was handed a large, brown paper bag full of peanuts straight out of the field. That is all—peanuts! As we drove home through the dark night, I teased him that he had "preached for peanuts." We did enjoy boiling them and having them for supper the next night.

Another weekend, we had made a long drive to a church, there were no gas stations open en route home, so we were running on empty. After midnight, nothing was open anywhere and every house was dark, the road narrow, and we were so nervously praying. We were plotting what to do WHEN we ran out of gas. Truly, I had never prayed as fervently or sincerely as I did that night. All got very quiet in the car. Charles was driving and coasting as much as possible. Just when things looked darkest we crested a hill and there was the southern part of Macon with lights on at gas stations. Both of us said a prayer of thanksgiving as we coasted into the first one! God never let us down. NEVER.

Other such opportunities led us into areas where we had never traveled and into cultures that we could only admire. Some of the churches were small mission churches, just getting a start in unchurched areas; others were established, big, and beautiful churches with efficient organizations and people who were thrilling to visit. Some were on the Southern Gulf coast where we could see the effects of so many hurricanes and learned why the people all lived in temporary dwellings. We traveled to one preaching opportunity via a motor boat, leaving our car at a parking lot. I was wearing high heels and Charles had on his coat and tie when we climbed into that small boat. The way to the tiny church took us through the bayous where we saw live alligators and large snapping turtles. Another Sunday we traveled up a highway that followed the Mississippi River north past several spillways used during flooding season and alongside canals. Then we went to a large town where we felt so at home, the building was just like our home church, and the people were so warm and friendly. These were highpoints in our lives and prepared us to understand and enjoy the diversity of people with whom we would minister for the rest of our lives.

Pearlington Baptist Chapel

Another supply Sunday led to a call to serve the Pearlington Baptist Chapel pastorate in Pearlington, Mississippi. This was a very small town on the Louisiana Mississippi border right on the Pearl River. The community was overwhelmingly Catholic, of French extraction and real bayou country. The beautiful little town boasted moss hung old trees, iron fenced yards full of exotic flowers, small, trim clapboard houses, small businesses that looked to be a century old, and some of the finest people one could ever encounter. The church was a mission of the First Baptist Church of Biloxi, Mississippi and really struggling. The membership was small, the building wee, the supplies negligible, funds did not exist. Yes, the challenge was tremendous! The people were so wonderful that falling in love with them and their little white stucco church was the most logical thing in the world.

We had great lessons of humanity in this church. Some of the people came to church by boat—for some a motor boat, but more likely a canoe, some even the picturesque dugout canoes that we had only seen in National Geographic magazines. Some of the men worked on the oil wells out in the Gulf of Mexico and were gone for weeks at a time. The women and the children managed to make their way to the little church to worship nevertheless. The language of the people was often broken English with French inserted. They called in "Cajun." In this new language which was musical, lilting, and very beautiful, they would describe the most mundane things making them seem so romantic and wonderful. One woman with whom I became very good friends, hugged me at the church door and said, "Don't worry, honey, I'm just a "bugaloo from Bayou Poh Poh." I would hear that designation over and over again, while I never understood what it meant, I always found it to be so picturesque.

The cooking was out of this world. Again, they called it Cajun or Creole. Whatever it was, it was outstanding! Although, I knew in my heart that I could never duplicate it, I tried to gain the wisdom that went into it and even asked for recipes. When I did so, the women looked at me askance because none of them used directions. Instead, they used a pinch of this, a bit of that, a handful of the other. There were all kinds of pasta dishes, crab used in so many ways that it challenged our use of hamburger in college, and fish—all kinds of fish—prepared with all kinds of spices, some from out in those swamps. Most everything was highly spiced, but so delicious! Some of the homes served their meals at a kitchen table with mismatched dishes; others made it a festive affair with decorations, a dining area/room, and fine china; and, still others prepared plates and served guests who then went about the house or outside if the weather was good to enjoy the meal. No matter, it was always wonderful! Red beans and rice (which I DID learn to make and which my children still enjoy), spaghetti sauce of the Gods, fried okra, catfish stew, oyster roasts, crawfish cooked outside, and the best cornbread you could ever eat. My favorite pie is Macaroon Pie which I learned to make there. Oh my, how I wish that I could duplicate those dishes. We had several church suppers where everyone brought food. Most of the time, we had no idea what we were eating, but we thoroughly enjoyed it.

With no lay leadership in the church, there was a constant struggle to create an organization with the tools and units necessary to meet the needs of this small congregation. Charles was totally committed: he visited, witnessed, and preached from his heart. Obviously, he was meeting with some success for one night as he was preaching, a young man came into the back of the tiny building yelling at him, to stop, to get out, to meet him outside, and shouting obscenities at the people in the congregation. This man was well known to the congregation because some of the men called him by name and immediately tried to subdue him while some of the others grabbed Charles and hustled him out past the man into our car where he was told to lock the doors. He did. The man got away from those seeking to restrain him and went to the car beating on it and yelling at Charles, even shaking it so that I feared it would turn over. Through all of this, I must admit that I cowered in the church behind some of the women in fear that this man would realize that I was "the preacher's wife" and come after me. (I am not really proud of that!) Finally, some Mississippi State Patrol deputies appeared, took the man into custody, and drove away with him after ascertaining that Charles was alright. Only then did I slip out of my hiding place and go to my husband. (Shame on me, I know.) We learned that the man was an enemy of religion as a whole and resented this place being in "his town." Apparently, he had done this before, but, he never did it again. That was a scary time.

To demonstrate the needs of this community, let me share with you that in addition to teaching a Sunday school class, I even played the piano for worship services! My mother had insisted that my sister and I take lessons, but I have no natural rhythm in my body whatsoever. I can read music a little bit so, I was pressed into duty. The Bible says, "Make a joyful noise" and that is what I did! Oh me, as I remember this I am humiliated.

We did see some minor gains, but nothing prepared us for leading a Vacation Bible School. The Pearlington Church had never had a Bible

School, so we did not know what to expect. With no funds, we were limited in our preparations. However, as we were learning, when God puts a person in a place, He gives them the tools to do His work, even if they come from some unexpected sources. At this time, I was working full time for the U. S. Army, so I had applied for leave to help with Vacation Bible School. However, my leave was cancelled due to an alert, and I was not going to be able to help. At first, I was outdone. This was the first time that there had been such an intrusion in my life when I was unable to do what I felt I was supposed to do. However, there was no alternative. We needed for me to keep this job to stay afloat in New Orleans so that Charles could complete his studies. The pay from the small church was negligible, the experience beyond value!

Borrowing materials from the Biloxi First Baptist Church we had made our own pupils' books. Preparing for twenty children (a very optimistic number) was a prayerful and time consuming task not to mention expensive. But, we managed.

The first morning of the School, I spent at my desk in my office in constant prayer. At noon, Charles called with the news that fifty children had enrolled! All of my Catholic coworkers pitched in and our Deputy Commander gave us the time to put together additional pupil books.

The Commanding Officer contributed the funds to purchase the paper to make thirty pupils' books. That evening we gathered other supplies using our funds and the donations from our friends. The next day was a repeat performance when more than eighty pupils enrolled in the Bible School. With the help of these friends we were able to financially and physically meet the needs of those pupils—all of them.

Each day refreshments were furnished. One day there was an ample supply of root beer and cookies. One little fellow kept coming back to Charles and in his French English Cajun dialect babbling something. Each time, Charles would refill his cup with root beer. After numerous trips, his sister came with him. Hearing the gibberish, Charles reached for the root beer, whereupon she said, "No, Sir, he's been telling you he needs to go to the bathroom!"

Over a hundred people came to the Commencement. There were too many to get into the building. Some stood outside and watched through the windows. Gnats, sand fleas, heat, lack of space, money and all, Pearlington taught us to utilize ALL of what one has and never underestimate the work of the Lord.

One of the things that was engraved upon my heart and soul about the church was the sheer determination on the part of the people. Because of their heritage, they were not accustomed to having many physical things. The world and all of its fads and material things was not important to them. Their primary goal was to exist and to provide an existence for their families. Whether that home was a red brick cottage in the village or a plywood hut in the swamp, it was theirs— they earned it and they protected it. Some of them were fishermen and because of the seasonality of that job, there were times of plenty and times when there was not as much; but, they were the most generous and giving people. They gave of themselves, their love, their hopes, and their dreams. They shared what belonged to them: many a Summer Sunday, we would leave at night for home with all kinds of fresh vegetables in our trunk which would provide most of our meals for the week. They grew the best tomatoes that I have ever eaten and were thrilled when I told them so. Yes, the legacy of these people has stayed with me in the decades since we left there. I believe that it always will.

We left Pearlington when Charles graduated from the Seminary. The leave taking was nostalgic. While we looked to our future with great optimism, we also looked at Pearlington with gratitude and wonder. These people did so much with so little and rejoiced through it all. Their joy was contagious and lives with me still. We felt secure in our future but we frankly wondered what the future of that little town and that church would be. Years later, Charles was invited back to the groundbreaking for a new building. To see the strides that those people had made was so rewarding. Then, NASA came in and took over the entire area to test the Saturn 5 rocket engines. Three small communities, each with a Baptist church, combined. One church had money, a second had people, and Pearlington had property. The result was a lovely white columned red brick building with a full time Pastor on the field living in a church built Pastor's home, and a good strong work. Again, he was invited back for Homecoming when the three churches occupied their new building. What a triumphant time for the witness of God in that place.

Then came Katrina—the hurricane that decimated New Orleans also overtook the tiny town and the church. There on the banks of the Pearl River the tide rose and rose and the wind and the rains came with it and the entire town was wiped out. The aftermath saw the God fearing and serving people spread in all directions. Most lost everything that they owned: some lost their lives trying to preserve a time honored way of living in the swamps. The only testimony to the little church where we learned so much is the concrete slab of that first tiny sanctuary where God blessed us all. Disaster? Yes, in many ways it is: but, in the depths of my soul, I know that scattered about those swamps some of those people and their descendants still live and I pray that their faith is still strong. The life that they lived and taught us how to live still vibrates deep within me. That cement slab may be all that is left physically, but the love of God and His offer of salvation are still available. The joy of life of those people is still there in the bent trees, rerouted river, and swamps that do still stand and have left their mark in ways that cannot be seen, only remembered with great thanksgiving.

Nicholls Baptist Church

This was our first church after Seminary. The location is in deep South Georgia, west of Savannah. The town was small but had everything that was needed. There was a bank, grocery store, appliance store, drug store, beauty shop, clothing store, you name it, we had it all. The church was on the edge of town located on a huge lot that covered a full city block. Typical Baptist architecture, it is red brick with white trim, round white columns across the front, and a white steeple with a large educational building across the back. The folks take very good care of the building and yards. They are proud of their church and respect its place and what it represents. The side and back yards are all huge old oak trees that provide the best shade in the word for dinner on the grounds.

Charles had been talking with the Pulpit Committee of this church for about three weeks before we came home for Christmas. While at my parents, we received a phone call suggesting that we detour en route back to Louisiana, and that he preach a trial sermon for the church. We cut our time with our family short and did this. We found the people to be wonderful and the church in excellent shape. The weekend there was wonderful.

Within two weeks of our return to New Orleans, we got the word that Charles had received the formal call to serve as their Pastor. We knew then that our lives were going to be quite different. This was the real thing—a career in the making. So, we moved from New Orleans to Nicholls—over a thousand miles—with all of our worldly possessions.

This Pastor's home was small but such a great home. We had three bedrooms, a living room with a fireplace, a real dining room with a built in china cabinet, a large kitchen and on the back, a glassed in porch that served as a laundry room and breakfast room and opened to the one bathroom. The front porch was straight out of my dreams: each end of it was a trellis where wisteria bloomed in the spring and summer. Across the dirt road from the front of the house was a hog pen! Black and white Poland hogs were our neighbors. In my dreams sometime, I still hear that feeder banging as they fed themselves in the middle of the night.

Here, I learned to be a full time housewife. I taught a coed adult Sunday school class that really kept me on my toes. We met in the choir loft after a Sunday school assembly each Sunday. This was a really great opportunity for me. We had a good group who were outgoing, ready to visit, see the church grow, and while doing so have a good time. They liked to eat, so we had many dinners—some of the time at the church and some of the time at various homes. This was great for socializing with couples our age.

One Sunday they decided to host a "covered dish dinner" for the church family. Still getting my feet under me as a housewife, I undertook to make a pound cake. Laboring long and measuring carefully, I was on the way to a masterpiece when I decided to save a step and break my eggs directly into the bowl of batter as it spun on the mixer table. First four eggs went with no problem, and then I dropped half of a shell with the fifth egg. Of course, the beaters broke it to smithereens and try as I might, I could not get all of the tiny pieces of shell out of the batter. There was no time to run to the store and start over. Besides, there was a lot already done for this cake. So, I just put the other ingredients in and baked it. Sure that the shell had dispersed throughout the batter, I proudly took my cake.

One of the lovely ladies came up to me afterward and said, "I never thought of adding nuts to pound cake batter. But, I enjoyed it. You are very bright!" I took the compliment and never said a word. From that day until this, I NEVER break eggs directly into anything!

This church was important to us for many reasons. We brought both of our sons home to the Pastor's home here. The home to which our second son came was brand new and marvelous. So, we learned how to handle a building program here. For six years we lived in Nicholls and enjoyed it so much. But, God spoke and the time came to move on to His next challenge for us.

Unadilla Baptist Church

We left deep South Georgia and moved north to Middle Georgia where we lived for the next six years. This town was somewhat larger and located right alongside the interstate highway. There were grocery stores, restaurants, furniture store, schools, and just about anything that you could name. The town was unique in that it had a sort of "Patron Saint." Judy Canova, a comedienne of the fifties had visited the town and fallen in love with its unique Indian name. She referred to it often in her act and visited often. When the engineers were laying out the interstate, they detoured AROUND the town because the Superintendent was a fan of Ms.

Canova.   So instead of being split by the highway, there were two exits from the Interstate to Unadilla.

This town had experienced a devastating tornado a couple of years before we moved there, so they had a relatively new and modern building. Not at all like the traditional buildings to which we were accustomed, but very sleek and modern. The auditorium was lovely. The Pastor's home was right next door with only the width of a driveway separating. This was quite convenient for shepherding three children through the rain to church, but our children, understanding that the house was a part of the church, would often bring all of their class to the house to use the bathroom or get water if the bathroom at church was crowded. Now, I did not mind this. I was proud of them for thinking about it. But, the problem came when they decided to play cars or look at books, or the like. Then, one of the mothers would have to go and round them up and march them into church late.

The swing set in our backyard attracted the little girls who would swing and slide and be let into church looking a bit worst for the wear as well. When the new Pastor's home was built on the next block, this sort of thing stopped. Oh we still had all of the children over in our yard, but not as often. Time would not permit.

The house was a small red brick one with three tiny bedrooms, a living room and a dining room and two wonderful glassed in rooms—one on either end of the front of the house. One of these became my sewing room and the other a little den for the boys. The kitchen was great with built in cabinets for the first time in my marriage. There was a small laundry room at the back with a small fenced yard for the children and a great clothes line for my use.

Here, we brought home our daughter and after a couple of years and another building program, we moved into the greatest house—a four bedroom, three bathroom home with a living room, dining room, den, GREAT kitchen, a bonus room for my sewing, and a half bath for the children who populated our back yard. This beautiful home was on a corner lot with a huge lawn. This was living at its greatest for me.

While here we had many guests much to the chagrin of our children who never quite understood this thing of "your best behavior." Once when we had the Georgia Baptist Women's Missionary Union Director and her friend to come for a missions emphasis and the boys had to give up their room for them, we really had the chance to explain what it meant to be the "Church's Family." That designation became a part of their lingo for some time for they understand it as a way to share. Those guests associated with two little boys who were not only "on their best behavior" but eager to behave and to be generous.

When we had some of our seminary friends, now missionaries to Venezuela, for a missions program, and they brought their boys. My children were in heaven. But, they were still little angels. They had learned to share their home and that was a good thing.

When after six years, God led Charles to leave Unadilla for a church north east of where we were, the children had problems understanding. But, at last they realized that this would be a new adventure—and it was!

By this time, we had acquired a dog and a cat along with three children and two cars. After the movers had loaded us up, we set out for our new home where they were going to meet us and unload on the same day. What a mistake that was!

I was driving one car with the cat and our daughter. Charles was driving the other with the boys and the dog. He was leading and I was to follow. All went well until we were about an hour into the trip when he put on his flashers and motioned me to pull over. When I did, we learned that the dog had thrown up in Charles's shoe! The boys thought it was hilarious. The car smelled terrible. So, the dog was moved to my car and the cat to his car. This upset the boys, so they moved to my car as well. What a trip that was!

Twin City Baptist Church

Arriving at the church, the moving van was right behind us. They were driving slower, but they had not had to make the stop that we did. Immediately, we began to unload our things as the church family showed up to help. By the end of that tiring day, the boys had made friends and already were riding their bikes around the town. Things were looking good!

What a fabulous little town this was. The church was older and of an architecture that had been popular at the turn of the century. The educational building was a plain brick two story building that served very well. Again, the Pastor's home was directly beside the church with only a driveway separating. This home was almost a replica of the first house in Unadilla even down to the two sun porches. The master bedroom did have its own bathroom which was nice. Directly across the street was the Primitive Baptist Church, so on Sunday this was a busy part of town.

The high school was just at the end of our street. Michael came home from school one day very upset because in his Math class all of the students were watching Charlaine ride her bicycle. She had one of those long flexible plastic sticks with a flag on the top mounted to the back of the bike. They could not see her, but they could see the flag going round and round and up and down all during their class. Michael was so embarrassed.

Here too, Charlaine broke her arm. She had climbed up into a dogwood tree in the yard beside our neighbor's driveway and could not get down by herself. She was about three years old. Michael was riding his bike around and around the block. She called to him to come and help her as he rode beneath the tree. He said, "Oh, OK, I will get you down just let me finish riding my bike." When he got back, she had fallen out of the tree and broken her arm. He was so upset and took full blame for it. She never forgave him even after they were adults. Always ready to remind him, she kept him on his toes.

While we were here, Mark had to have an emergency appendectomy. That day, I was substitute teaching when the school called Charles that Mark was sick. No knowing what to do, he went to get Mark, brought him home and turned on the TV. By the time school was out and I got there, Mark was absolutely green and so sick. Sending Charlaine and Mike to the church and their father I took Mark to the doctor who sent us straight to the hospital for emergency surgery. I was with him at the hospital when Charles brought Mike and Charlaine in to see him. Charlaine got up under his hospital bed and was playing with her doll, totally unaware that her brother had almost died. Mark was still out cold. Mike was bending over him saying, "Is he gonna die, Daddy? Is he gonna die?" At that very time, the anesthetic wore off and poor Mark—the first thing he saw was Michael's face and heard his question. That is something that he never forgot. Poor Mike, he seemed to always be in the right place at the wrong time and create these situations.

Twin City was a good experience. The people were wonderful. The town was just the right size and convenient to everything. There was an excellent music and Women's Missionary Union program. In fact, the youth program was so good that we took two choir trips. We would rent a bus and stay in the homes of church members where we were singing. We took a trip to Washington, D.C. where we laid a wreath at the tomb of the Unknown Soldier and sang in the amphitheater of Arlington Cemetery. We also were the guests of President Nixon at the White House when he welcomed the Japanese Ambassador.

The next year we went to New Orleans and met some really great people on the way there and back. We stayed in the dorm at the New Orleans Seminary so it was a sweet reunion for us. While we traveled with the choir the children would stay with some of the church members or the grandparents would come and get them for a week. These times were kind of like a vacation if you can call it that when you travel with a busload of teenagers.

After three years, God again led Charles to a new opportunity where someone strong in missions awareness and willingness was needed badly. So, we left Twin City and headed north to Covington, Georgia.

High Point Baptist Church

This was an amazing experience. High Point was in a building program. On one side of the Jackson Highway was the Pastor's home up on a hill behind the cemetery and behind the original church building. On the other side was the new church building. Only the basement had been finished and it was gorgeous. Out front was a big tennis court, and behind the church was a baseball field. The inside was all modern and clean with lots of glass. The long term program called for building the traditional red brick, white columned sanctuary atop this basement in about ten years.

The Pastor's home was across the highway on a hill behind the old church and educational facility beside the cemetery. Again, it was red brick with three bedrooms, two bathrooms, a living room, dining room and a very nice kitchen, den and laundry room. There was a small front porch as well. The lawn was all downhill toward the highway with fruit trees. The highway was a busy one, but with the old educational building in front, the noise was negligible.

The most interesting thing there was the Bus Ministry. Because the church was not far from Jackson Lake—a very large fishing lake where many people had cabins right on the lake—there were many people who actually lived there with many children and no church at all. So, every Sunday morning the church would send two buses down to the lake and return loaded with children and adults who wanted to attend church. This was an expensive ministry and it took some men and women who were really dedicated to keep it going, but they did. So many professions of faith came from that group. Sunday night baptism was a routine thing. Many of these young people stayed in the area and grew up in that church thanks to the bus ministry.

The buses also ran for Vacation Bible School and this was a real treat. We had many children of all ages who would get the bus and come to Bible School. Our facilities were more than adequate for we could take over the whole building. There was money in the budget to provide enough literature for all of these children along with refreshments and the bus transportation. Graduation night, the buses would bring back not only the children but the parents and grandparents as well. This was a real evangelistic opportunity. We could see the Great Commission at work here.

Here we put into being the Backyard Bible Clubs which were wildly successful. Our own children got to the point that they were able to help in these. One of the reasons they were such good helpers was that they went to several of them each summer and were of an age where they could really be useful. We were able to reach many, many children in the neighborhood around the church as well as when we went to the lake. We reached the older children this way. Several times, we also were able to minister to the parents of the neighbors where we were holding the Clubs. This was a wonderful ministry.

There was a large wooded area behind our house. The boys loved camping out there. They had their tent and sleeping bags and would go off to the woods night after night. When we moved from there, the thing that Michael missed most was the woods and camping out. Long after Michael was an adult, he would recall these adventures and say that this was the best time of his life.

Charlaine liked playing in a little shed out back. She made it a playhouse and enjoyed walking and "exploring" the woods. She began school while we lived here.

A few years ago I was driving to Macon and got off of the Interstate and drove through Covington and down by High Point. Now they have the sanctuary built atop that basement and it is beautiful red brick with white columns and a beautiful lawn where the boys played baseball. They have torn down the old church and you can see the Pastor's home from the highway. Unfortunately, there are more graves in the cemetery but from the looks of things some of those kids grew up to take pride in that church. I was thrilled to see it.

We spent three years there—all of them wonderfully fruitful and fulfilling. Apparently we had done the task for which God intended, because He called Charles to lead another church.

Cobbtown Baptist Church

Back to deep South Georgia! This was an interesting setup. The town was not very big, but the outlying farms made it huge. The principal crop was tobacco and seeing all of those tobacco houses was a new experience for us. We moved in March. The movers were late getting us

loaded and we had three vehicles to get to
Cobbtown. So just as it was getting dark we set
out: I was driving my car with Charlaine and a
dog: Michael who had a learner's permit only
was driving the little van with Mark as his
copilot, and Charles brought up the rear in his car
with the cat. What a parade we made.

There was no place to stay in Cobbtown, so we
had put some mattresses and blankets in the van.
When we got to the Pastor's home, we unloaded
those and put them in the Master Bedroom and
we spent our first night like that as a family.
When we got there, the boys were hungry—as
usual—and I had packed some food for them, but
on the kitchen counter was a freshly baked pound
cake with a note reading, "Welcome Home."
There was milk in the fridge, so they were quite
happy.

The movers awoke us the next morning. Despite
the fatigue and the strangeness of our setup, we
had all had a good night's sleep. The children
were anxious to get up and explore their new
home. We were eager to get the movers to work
so that we could begin a new ministry.

This move was particularly interesting. When a
moving company loads a family's belongings,
they put all of the packed boxes neatly in first.
Then they put in the furniture with some boxes in
and around it. Then at the very back, sometimes

even hanging off of the back is all of the junk: bicycles, swing set, yard tools, trampoline, and lawn mower, all of the stuff that just looks plain bad. The ladies of the church along with some of the men always show up to help unpack, set up the kitchen and help with everything else. Naturally, they are curious as to what this family has, what kind of furniture, how much, etc. Well, what they see is the junk! In our case the first thing to come off was the basketball goal which was a telephone pole with the goal attached that had been buried in red dirt. Then off came the trampoline in pieces. I was so embarrassed. But the children just started assembling their things in the yard and finally the movers got to the good stuff. But, that is always a problem and, I guess because of the ages of the children, this one was really bad with all of the red dirt on the basketball goal pole, the plethora of bicycles and outdoor equipment, it was just bad!

The church building in Cobbtown was made of yellow ceramic blocks. The architecture was turn of the century which gave it real character. Concrete steps came out of the front and continued on both sides of the portico at the front of the church. The Pastor's home was next door separated by a sandy parking lot with lovely huge oak trees. The home was large, having been added onto considerably. We had four bedrooms, formal living room, dining room, nice kitchen and great pantry, fabulously huge den with a great fireplace and a master suite with plenty of closet space, its own bathroom and a dressing room. The den and master suite were the add ons. Across the road was a huge tobacco field as far as the eye could see. In the summer it was emerald green and working alive with harvesters. The church was the last building on the road that came through town and continued on to the next town. Normally there was little traffic; but, in the summer this was a busy place.

The yard was very nice, with a great lawn and trees. The front yard was neat and easy to keep. There was a small screened porch off to the side in the front that was the perfect place in the spring and fall. Behind us were great neighbors with a son Michael's age. They planted a huge garden each summer and we were the happy recipients of some of the goods.

Oh my, at the experiences that we had there. Because the boys were both teens there, we had constant traffic in our home. The youth program was excellent with some fine young people who enjoyed their church. The WMU program was well founded and the ladies seemed to really enjoy it. Here, I taught a Men's Bible Class that met in the sanctuary. Now, this was really an experience. In my class were most of the deacons and the wonderful older men of the church. I thought that it would be temporary but it became permanent. We had delightful times together.

Because we lived on a county line, the children went to school in the neighboring country where the schools were closer than if they had to go to our county seat. This meant that one of us had to take them to the bus at the county line each morning and meet them in the afternoon. That turned out to be less of a burden and more of an opportunity to be alone for a bit. I would take my Bible and Sunday school book and study while I waited. This was also a time to pray, really pray for nothing interrupted. I began to anticipate these times.

God had in mind that this church would meld into an amicable group of folks that would not divide by age group, social class, or any of the other divisions that can exist. Instead, these people were led to come together and experience what God could really do when His people were willing. Prayer meetings were wonderful times of true worship. Church suppers were so well attended. The young people made Sunday Evening services their choice. They would bring their dates and fill up the back rows of the church. That was a very rewarding sight for those of us with teenagers in our homes.

The people of Cobbtown were wonderful. There were a number of couples with children the age of ours and they all seemed to get along so well. Many great things came out of our time there. Both of the boys graduated from high school, and Charlaine entered middle school. Both boys began dating and Charlaine wished that she could. Yes, these were halcyon days.

We were there for six years. Michael was in his third year of college; Mark was graduating when God again came with a call to move along. By this time, I was teaching full time in a neighboring town with a contract. So, when we received the call to move, I had to stay behind and teach out my contract. Mark, Charlaine and I had a little house in the neighboring town where they commuted back to Metter to school, and I went to my school each day. On weekends, we would leave as soon as school was out and go to our new home where Charles was living full time and pastoring the church. We did that from February until school was out in June. This was difficult, but when God calls, He gives the directions and the energy to make it work. And, it does.

Union Grove Baptist Church

So, we moved the north. This would be our first time to be near where we had both grown up. By this time, the culture had changed so much that it was hardly like coming home. We would have only one child in school here. Mark was entering college in the fall and spending his summer at the Royal Ambassador Camp as a counselor. Michael had a job as well. So, this was a unique move. We were sort of returning to the way we had started out.

Although we had no way of knowing it, this would be our last church. Here are precious memories of some truly great folks and some wonderful times. First, these people hired a truck and a group of men came to Cobbtown and moved us to Lithia Springs. They were marvelous—not so happy when they saw the piano, but they managed.

Lithia Springs is just West of Atlanta and the little unincorporated town is very convenient. Mail is delivered; there are international chain grocery stores and restaurants. Yes it is fine. The town is located on the Interstate 20 which makes it very convenient to get into Atlanta or wherever.

Picking out the best thing is difficult. The Pastor's home was located across a canyon from the church in thick trees which afforded privacy to the max. The church was the traditional red brick with columns, and an educational building. The old church still stood and had the most beautiful stained glass windows you can imagine. Worship was easy in this new church where the huge windows were clear class and the trees and sky just came into the sanctuary. Down in the canyon, the men had built a pavilion which was perfect for youth meetings and the like. At one time the stream that was tiny then, had been deep enough to hold baptizing. I would love to have seen that. These people were happy with their building and loved their church. There was always someone there doing something to assure comfort and good repair. My hat is off to them for that.

When we moved there we had a beautiful blonde retriever mix dog. She was the best dog. Charlaine had trained her and she made every step that Charlaine made. When she was in school, Duchess would go to the study with Charles and lay outside on the porch all of the time he was there. But, when Charlaine came home, she would go home to be with her. She was beloved by all of us but she wanted to be a Baptist dog. We had a time with her. On Sundays when the church door opened, she would come right in just like she belonged. She would greet people and wander down the aisle if one of us did not catch her. The boys were good about getting her and taking her home. We locked her up before we would leave, but she always seemed to get out and when she did, she went to church. The people were really good about it. Everyone knew Duchess.

One of the interesting events at Union Grove were the monthly Sunday night fellowships. For one of these occasions, they decided that there would be a contest to see which man would make the best cake. The rules were simple: the man must do ALL of the work on his cake and bring it for the judging that Sunday night where it would become our dessert. Several men signed up, including Charles. Now, he has NEVER cooked. He knew where the kitchen was but had no clue as to its purpose. We had recently purchased a crock pot (I believe that we call them slow cookers now) which came with a little recipe book which was for a cake! Yes, a Crock Pot Cake. This was his intention. I made sure that we had all of the ingredients, showed him where the implements were and set the crock pot out for him. He took over after that. He hovered over that crock pot like a mother hen over her little chickens. Proudly he took it to the church that night (it had a very unusual appearance). No, he did not win. In fact, his cake was deemed by the judges and the attendees as the "Worst Cake" there. He never baked again!

We were there for six years. Mark graduated from college and became employed. Michael began his career with the Georgia Department of Corrections as an Officer where he spent his entire career, retiring from there. Charlaine graduated from high school early and went to college in nearby Atlanta while living at home.

Charles lost his father and I lost my mother. Our lives were taking on new directions all of the time. The most miraculous thing was despite all of our changes, God was consistent. His love surrounded us, blessed us, and used Charles to facilitate the program and reach those who were lost or in need. God had been at work in that church for many years and the dedication of the people showed it.

I will always love the people of Union Grove. When Charles was so sick they really rallied around the children and me. They kept the children fed while I stayed at the hospital and would bring food to me there. They visited him and prayed with him, read the Bible with him, and truly loved him. They came out to the church in great numbers to say goodbye at his funeral and at the cemetery. These were truly God's people.

After the funeral in the days and weeks when I was struggling to get a grip on this new life of mine, they were more than kind to me. They actually became my family. Whenever I remember those hard, hard days, I have warm feelings for these great folks and how they surrounded my children and me when we needed it so badly.

Our ministry there ended after six years not as all the others had ended, but with the knowledge that

Charles had answered God's final call to him. The children and I were now to answer God's call on our own.

In reviewing these times in all of these churches with all of these people, I realize anew that in each succeeding church to which God led us He challenged the best that we possessed. Incidents of great humor, pathos and inspiration were unique in their certainty. As years passed, we came to see that God's work is challenging, calling for a regular return to total commitment, and a regular acknowledgement of the leadership of God. Accepting that challenge to total surrender proved to be the cornerstone on which we were able to move out into the mainstream of God's plan for our life together.

When Jesus assembled His disciples and other followers together to teach them, He must have looked out upon them just as we looked at each of our congregations, wondering "Now, what is God going to give us to do together? What kind of task does He have in mind for them to accomplish? Who will He pick to be the leader? Who will have the best ideas? Where are those who will do the music? On whom will He depend to visit and seek out the lost? And me, oh God, me, just what do you have in mind for me here in this place? These people have needs great and small. I cannot know them all; but, I want to know them—all of them. We just have to work together under the leadership of the Holy Spirit to do His will."

Churches are more than buildings—brick, mortar, sheet rock and paint. Churches are made up of people who are doing their very best to be Christians. They want to live good lives and bring in their fellow man. They want to glorify God. When God calls the right leader to the right church and the people are the right people, everything is wonderful. We were lucky enough to see that happen over and over. Really, I am incorrect when I call our path "lucky." We were following what the Holy Spirit led us to do. He found the need and sent us to that place. Oh, what great people we met! How I look forward to seeing them all again in heaven! How thankful I am to have been with His people and to worship Him as God.

"I thank him who has given me strength for this, Christ Jesus our Lord, because he judged me faithful by appointing me to his service.
-        I Timothy 1:12

A Confluence of Paths

Two roads diverged in the middle of my life,
                I heard a wise man say
I took the road less traveled by
And that's made the difference every night and
                every day.
Larry Norman

(With apologies to Robert Frost)

Chapter Four

Building a Life

With the conclusion of seminary, it seemed that all of the seven years of our marriage had been preparing us for this time. Suddenly, it seemed that the light had changed from yellow to green. It was time to GO! Or, like someone had yelled, "Ready, set, GO!" The gears changed and our lives went into high. We were "grown up" all of a sudden and in charge of our lives. Oh wait! Were we in charge? While we could say "Yes" and "No" we remembered that we were under the leadership of the Lord and our destiny was in His hands. But, now, all preparations were made and we were ready to begin the task He put before us for real!

The Pastorates into which God led us were increasingly demanding. Each had its contribution to make to our life. In retrospect, I realize that these churches gave us so much more than we ever gave to them. They gave us experiences on which we could continue to build our lives in God's service. Each put a very important building block into the structure that would become our legacy.

God led us back to our home state, Georgia, after Seminary and to a fabulous full time Pastorate in an established church. This was a small town on the plains of the southern part of the state where the winters were comparatively mild and the summers so hot that they were unbelievable. On our first visit, we were impressed by the church grounds, large and landscaped, taking up a full block. The building itself was traditional red brick with white columns and a sizable educational building as well. The church just looked like it belonged where it was. The people were so good to us, even on that first visit. What a miracle happens when God leads His people to one another!

Early in this time of our lives, soon after moving to Nicholls, we became parents with all of the subsequent problems, joys, and opportunities. The major problem was maintaining my full schedule of church activities, being a wife to Charles and also being a good parent. Had I been a young bride, new to the life of Ruth, I wonder how I might have coped. Our first child, a son, was reared on the back row of the church. We had no church nursery. While he was an infant, this was not a problem: with a bottle and a pacifier, I could count on him going to sleep and all would be well. But, when he got beyond that stage, he tuned in more to what was happening and had so many questions. A problem arose when he was just beginning to talk and accustomed to being admired for his words. Just because he was ours, he felt that the people in the church needed to know that he was there. He began to spontaneously let out the most blood curdling scream—just one, but it was enough. All eyes turned to us. Humiliated I shushed him; but, he was fine, he had enjoyed his moment and went back to his cars. As this continued into later months, he and I would make a trip outside for discussion about what we did and did not do in church. Such was his life. Gradually, he realized that when in that sanctuary he was to be quiet and attentive. But, getting him to that stage was not without frazzled nerves.

Poor kid, he went to more missionary circle meeting than most of our ladies. Once, I taught a mission study with him playing on the floor at my feet. He just accepted that is what we were doing that day and coped with it. He had his cars and books and a new location so, to him, it was all good! When he was a baby and teething, I had an obligation to teach a study, so I bundled him up and took him with me teaching while holding him in my arms or on my hip. Often I asked myself, "Why?" Keeping my schedule was important to me, but he was important too. I could only hope that I was not ruining him for church in his future. The night that he was baptized, I realized that those years had been well spent. We were so pleased with Mike's salvation experience. The church was a real part of his life. This was a startling discovery when he became an adolescent.

Our son began to chafe a bit at "so much church" when he was about eight years old. After a soul searching conference, his father and I explained to him that church attendance was optional. God's house should be a house of joyful worship, not of compulsory attendance. We enumerated our own happiness in worship and our experiences as children. Sitting in the authoritative position of adult, we looked back at "If I had only known. . ." Mike listened to all of this respectfully and when his dad concluded, ". . . so, if you do not want to go to church and Sunday school, you do not have to go. It is all up to you."

Wide eyed, Mike asked, "Really, daddy?"

Sunday came, and the family went off to church, all except Mike. Our hearts were so heavy—we were disappointed! Here we thought that we were such great parents and that we had handled the situation with such grace. We were humiliated. Five minutes into Sunday school, Michael walked in, dressed in his Sunday clothes and grinning broadly. No more chafing. He was free to choose, and basking in his responsible choice, he stood taller than before! No, those early years had not been wasted!

In later years, Mike repeated the lesson he had learned to his siblings and proudly led them to church himself. Our second son, Mark, and our daughter, Charlaine, did not chafe as Mike had done. I often wonder if that is because he had paved the way. Of course, when Mike became a young person, we had the lesson all over again. He was instrumental in getting many other boys into our church because he made the choice to come and repeated that choice to them. Seemingly, giving the opportunity to choose meant a lot to those children. More surprising, was their eagerness to make the right choice. I shall always believe that God led us to have that first talk with Mike and allowed good seed to be planted in the fertile field that was Mike's heart and soul. The harvest was to the glory of God in the lives that were touched by his example.

Rearing a child or children in the spotlight of "preacher's kids" is an experience that would take an encyclopedia to fill. I often wonder why the Seminary did not give lessons in doing that. At any rate, I enjoy looking back to the times when our children were babies. The church family accepted them and loved them with their whole hearts. Of course, there were loads and loads of gifts, and plenty of advice, but it was the acceptance into the church family that meant so much to me. Because we were never geographically near our families, our children did not have the luxury of visiting grandparents all of the time nor being indulged by aunts and uncles or getting to know their cousins. The loving attention of the church family gave them that so that they never knew that they were missing anything.   Other mothers would bring their children to Sunday school and church because they realized that I was there with mine. From this, we were able to develop a church nursery before Mark came along.

As the church family became the extended family for our children (so many "aunts" and "uncles") here were those older couples who became like the grandparents our children saw only a couple of times a year. These were often people whose own grandchildren lived far away and they played that part with our children as substitutes. In return, our children loved them and enjoyed visiting them and sharing their treasures as if these were their real grandparents. At any rate, this was a blessing because our children had the love of so many and grew up in a loving, trusting environment where they felt loved and wanted as well as safe and secure.

Of course, it was not always easy. There were times when the children "got in the way" of something or someone.   These were not comfortable times and fortunately they were few and far between.   There was always someone who felt that with the responsibilities we had in the church, that we did not need the children. We needed to "focus." Ah, me, if those folks only knew how we DID focus. Also, because our children were not perfect (whose are?) they sometimes caused problems.

We had a wonderful elderly lady who lived behind us when Michael first learned to walk. In her yard she had a cement frog which weighed about two or three pounds. She painted it a vivid green with yellow spots: it nestled beneath some of her shrubbery beside some beautiful flowers. She was not a member of our church, but she was very nice. In our walking about the neighborhood, somehow, Mike spotted that frog. He went up into the yard to pet it. I saw nothing wrong with that. After a little petting and some explaining from me about what a frog is, how it lives, and its purpose, he left it to continue our walk. The next day, I was hanging the clothes out to dry and he was playing in his sand box. When I was done and ready to go into the house, I was shocked to see that frog sitting in the sand box. Upon my inquiry, Mike told me that the frog was tired of that yard and wanted to play. Needless to say, I went with him to return it to the lady's yard. Next day it was back. That went on for some time. We punished him, explained about taking things, explained about the frog LIKING where it was sitting, and all of the other things we thought would get the message across. None did. Finally, when I went with Mike to take it back for the umpteenth time, the lady came out and told him that he could have the frog for his sand box. She told him that the frog had explained that it needed a little boy. The problem was solved and for the rest of his life he LOVED frogs.

One of our deacons lived next door to us. His grandchildren were all college age and he and Mike bonded over tractors. Mike loved tractors and when this wonderful man would come to take him for a ride, Mike was in heaven. Right then, he decided that he would become a farmer so that he could ride a tractor. This man had a garden separated from our yard by a big picket fence. When his watermelons were ripe, he would get up every morning early, pick one, and reach over the fence to roll it into our yard for Mike. That man became Mike's "Grandpa." The entire time that we served there, Mike and he would meet to discuss tractors and watermelons. He had so much patience with our little boy who was only three and four years old.

When the other children came along, they too made friends with church members in a special way. Mark was less outgoing than Mike, but he made friends with the guys who would play ball near our house. For hours, he would hang onto the fence watching them play baseball. The guys never minded and talked with him about the ball game, even giving him a ball of his own. Mark slept with that ball in his bed for years. Another of the men gave him an old baseball glove. Miles too big for Mark, he did not care. He would put on that glove and throw the ball. Of course he did not catch it, but he would spend hours all by himself throwing the ball while wearing the glove. Many years later, he had his own glove and played organized ball in high school.

Mark had no trouble in church. In the morning services, he was in the nursery; for the evening services, he and Mike sat with me on the back row. Unlike Mike, Mark loved the quiet and was happy with a book or a car for the entire time. Often, he would curl up against me and sit quietly. Everyone thought that he was the best child in the world! No other children were that mild and meek in church. Mike would try to involve him in games with the cars, or pick at him to aggravate him, but Mark just turned him away. At length, I learned to put Mike on one side and Mark on the other. Mark would play or sit quietly, and Mike would be under my control.

While Mark was a toddler, Mike was in Kindergarten. I was serving as Divisional Vice President of Georgia Baptist WMU which meant that I had to travel all over South Georgia for meetings and to teach. There was always a nursery provided, so I would pack Mark's bag and off the two of us would go. He loved to ride in the car so this was an adventure for him. He was not always cooperative about my leaving him in the nursery. Once, in Tifton, I could not leave him, he was just too pitiful. He was almost two at this time and such a sweet child. So, I picked him up and took him into the auditorium with me. He had no toys or books. But, he seemed to know that this was one of those times to be quiet, so he sat up against my side and watched everything that went on. When it was my turn to speak, he went with me and stood by my side like he was my assistant. He did go to the nursery after lunch so that he could nap.

Learning new things was not difficult for Mark; he just did not always do it when it was expected. For instance, walking: I had begun to believe that Mark would be crawling when he went to college, then all of a sudden, it happened. We were preparing to go to church. I had dressed him in his brand new all white suit (a gift from his Uncle Joel) and against his skin, it was gorgeous. I told him, "Too bad you will be crawling and get all of this so dirty—if only you would walk!" Those big, brown eyes just looked up at me like he understood. As I gathered my things, and went out into the hall, Mark crawled down from his bed, stood on his two feet firmly, lifted his hands for balance and walked! He just had to do it on his own time table. He did not crawl again, he walked and soon was running and jumping.

He was so easy to toilet train. Mike had been a real problem never having time to bother with it. I suppose that he remembered, because, he trained Mark in no time at all. Mike guided him in many other things at which he excelled early. Most of these were good, but Mike also taught him to get into mischief; however, Mark mastered the art of looking innocent far sooner than Mike.

Mark loved all people and they loved him. He was such a sweet child. When he made his profession of faith and was baptized at age eight, the entire congregation united in prayers for him. That is how much they loved him.

Charlaine was different from the boys. Their playing was different from hers and she had no sister. She would drive us crazy wanting to go to someone's house to play or have someone to our house to play. She had lots of little friends and their mothers were very cooperative to let their children come or to let Charlaine visit them. But, with the boys and their friends so close, she did become a tom boy. Much to the delight of some of the other mothers, she played football with the boys and was quite good. When she began playing the piano at age 3, that became more of a passion for her. The other children would love to come in and listen to her play and shout out things for her to play. She had a great talent and enjoyed doing it. Her first tune to master was "Bad, Bad, Leroy Brown." The boys loved bringing their friends in to hear that.

She, like Mike, was reared in the church services. I shall never forget the Christmas that she received the doll that she had requested from Santa. This was a special doll that when handled in a certain way would roll over and cry. The rolling over involved some kind of mechanical process that had gear grinding and made an awful noise. The crying was just plain crying. Christmas that year came on Sunday, so her taking the doll to church was discussed roundly. Her father told her not to take it. Somehow, she got it there. By the time I realized it, services had begun and I could not get it out. Sure enough, while Charles was preaching, she hit the wrong button and the doll started the cranking noise of rolling over. Humiliated, I grabbed the doll thinking to stop the rolling and mistakenly touched the button to make her cry. Needless to say, we got a dirty look from the pulpit!

So, the children were reared in the spotlight but it never really seemed to bother them. Occasionally they would wish that they could go to a certain place or stay home to see a certain TV program or the like. But, with some encouragement they honored the church. We always lived right at the church, so they had to keep their toys picked up and the yards free from "junk" which did annoy them. They were never bothered by the constant flow of people to the house day and night. They learned to go to their rooms and give their father and the guest privacy and not to ask questions. All in all, this was just more building blocks for us.

When Lilacs Last in the Dooryard Bloom'd

When lilacs last in the dooryard bloom'd,
And the great star early droop'd in the western
sky in the   night,
I mourn'd—and yet shall mourn with ever
returning spring.
O ever returning spring! Trinity sure to me you
bring;
Lilac blooming perennial, and drooping star in
the west,
And thought of him, I love.
O powerful, western, fallen star!
O shades of night! O moody tearful night!
O great star disappear'd! O the black murk that
hides the sky!
O cruel hands that hold me powerless! O
helpless soul of me!
O harsh surrounding cloud that will not free my
soul!
      Walt Whitman (1819 – 1882)

"Jesus wept!" (John 11:35 KJV)

Chapter Five

Little Bumps in the Road

As the years went by, we grew up, matured and gleaned from our everyday experiences the valuable lessons of member friendships, building programs, and involvement! Other lessons came into play with the bitter disappointments, frustrations, and countless blessings. All were building blocks for this unique task to which we had been called.

One of the things that I believe one can only learn by experience is to deal with disappointments—the little ones as well as the larger ones. I say this because, I believe this is what happened to me. Going into any experience with rose colored glasses is typical of inexperience and immaturity. My greatest disappointments came from misunderstandings, confusion, frustration and the movement into different areas where the norm was different to what I knew. The fact that all people are not what they seem to be was difficult for me to grasp and to learn to accept. Hypocrisy was (and still is) frustrating to me. Why be a hypocrite about what is going on in one's life. Accept it and move forward. Yet, I was often faced with the cruel truth that that is not the way that all of us interact. Then, expecting perfection was another of my disappointments. I was (and still am) so aware of the presence of Jesus Christ in my life, and the sinless perfection that He brings to me, that acknowledging that others had no problem with disappointing him was very hurtful to me. But, with time, I learned to cope with these things and to pray long and hard for the people with whom I was dealing and for myself as well. With God's help, I learned to accept people without trying to enumerate their shortcomings and to use our experiences together to help me grow.

In one Pastorate, we lived in a small town that offered no social life. The church was the center of the community. Everyone knew that I was the "preacher's wife," and treated me a bit differently than they treated one another. To many, I was a confessor, to others merely a necessary element, to some a discomfort, and to a few, a real person. I enjoyed all of these people, particularly the latter. At this time in my life, I learned the "danger" of having close, personal friends in a small town where you are the Pastor's wife.

At one time, I saw no problems with having a best friend, and had a close, warm friendship: we were neighbors and friends. Our ages were quite close and neither of us had children at that time. Our husbands were compatible and we had a great deal in common; therefore, we spent considerable time together. Her husband was a deacon in our church and she was very active. We had a wonderful relationship. This proved to be a source of much consternation in the church family. Unbeknownst to me, many of the older women resented the friendship feeling that we "shared too much of the church business" with our friends. Many of the young adults reacted negatively out of jealously I suppose, thinking that this couple was privy to "running the church."

Of course, none of this was true. We were simply friends. This couple filled a human need in our lives allowing us to be ourselves and share joys and sorrows. We shared love—fraternal love. This was a good time. Unfortunately, the negative feelings of the people of the community became known to us and affected our relationship. We did not alter our lifestyle, that would have been hypocritical, but when we left that Pastorate, we left off that happy time. There have been no more such close friendships. An invisible wall was built through which I have not let myself pass since that time. I have had good friends in all of our churches. I maintain them as we move on; but, there have been no more intimate friends and no obvious "best friend."

That has been my loss. Having grown up so close to my sisters and having had a best friend in high school, then making and holding relationships with so many of the sister Pastor wives in college and the seminary, this is really something that I have missed. In addition, there has been a very personal byproduct: my almost painful shyness returned. While some may have felt that I was indifferent, this experience coupled with my natural acute shyness has altered my life.

There is a strange paradox regarding individual personal friendships in the ministry. Cultivating a close and intimate friendship seems to breed enemies—literally the extremes. On the other hand, keeping one's distance, being warm, friendly, compassionate, and yet maintaining an obvious unilateral relationship breeds enthusiastic warmth and response. No one loses, except me. In divorcing myself from the closeness, I forego the emotional support of those upon whom I might rely. Yet, I gain security in knowing the far reaching positive effects. In reality, I benefit from the extended range of those who seek out my friendship. Besides, it is an attribute of Ruth, ". . . thy people shall be my people" (Ruth 1:16 KJV). Notice this is not singular but refers to the group.

A great lesson in life and in the ministry came with our first building program. In retrospect, the catastrophic and far reaching effects of a relatively ordinary business transaction never crossed my mind. But, then, we had never built a home or even bought a house; so, we were totally inexperienced. The decision to build a Pastor's home had been made some time prior to Charles assuming the Pastorate. In reality, the part that was ours to plan was administrative only. I cannot overemphasize the almost total lack of understanding on the part of the church people regarding the Pastor and the building program. There had to be no "personal" feelings involved at all.

For instance, the building committee was made up of six totally different people with diverse backgrounds, outlooks, financial ideas and church commitment. (The Pastor is an ex officio member of the committee.) To these people is given the task of developing a viable procedure. Directed by the church body to build a Pastor's home, they must select a construction plan that fits the financial climate of the church, projects the proper image, meets the needs of the Pastor family, not only at the present but of any future families, and keep within the makeup of the neighborhood/town. This responsibility cannot be taken lightly. When a family decides to build a home they have only to consider themselves and their physical needs. This committee had to remember that one former Pastor had six children and a plethora of furniture when he came to lead the church. In the past there had been a Pastor who was not even married. Another former Pastor came with a house full of family heirlooms, and another came with very little furniture and three children. So coming to the very first decision was quite demanding.

The next decision was finding a place to put the house. Right next door to the church is the traditional place for a Pastor's home; however, in recent years locating a Pastor's home a bit detached from the church has become more acceptable. If the church has a great deal of property, that helps the situation; but, if not, property has to be secured or, hopefully, donated. Then comes the problem of securing a contractor who can work within the church budget and present a Christian model of conduct for the community. The most controversial problem of all then arises: choosing every detail for the finishing of the house from paint colors, to floor covering, to light fixtures and on and on the list goes. This is a long, drawn out and often thankless task. The church members who undertake it give so much of themselves in time and energy while working so hard to keep conflicts to a minimum. The fact that there are those with the knowledge and know how to do this knowing what all is involved is amazing to me.

Thank goodness, few of the decisions utilize the Pastor's thinking, ideas, expertise, understanding or diversification for the task. Basically, his job is to keep peace within the church family and keep the project going. Nevertheless, overseeing and administration are challenging tasks in and of themselves.

Unfortunately, human nature being fallible, there are always church members who disagree on the basic issue of building in the first place, resent the expense, or neighbors, even family members whom they cannot criticize, so the logical one to blame is the Pastor. After all, he is responsible! And, so it goes—

We received our baptism of fire with the construction of a Pastor's home early in our ministry. As young marrieds, it was a tremendous ego trip to have a brand new home. The price was high, however. We endured months of planning with some bickering among the dissidents within the church. The committee suffered too, and for some of them there came a detachment from the program of the church. The heavy demands of a new building are expensive—physically, mentally, emotionally, and spiritually. I shall always have the greatest of respect for that Committee. They did their job so well and hung together leading the church in an important program. My love and respect for them knows no bounds.

We did play a part in this new building however. We had to purchase the new drapes, rugs to protect the hardwood, and other accessories. This was certainly necessary moving from a five room, one bathroom home to a nine room, two bath home with a toddler. Some had intimated that they expected high quality merchandise which was in keeping with the finishing touches of the building. We tried very hard to live up to the standards. I was deeply hurt when I completed sewing all of my new drapes and took them to hang in the new Pastor's home. As soon as I unlocked the door, I was joined by one of the Committee members who wanted to "inspect" my choice of fabric, choices of color, and workmanship. There was no overt criticism but also no words of encouragement. I resented this at first, but I also appreciated the dedication. In the ensuing years, I have come to realize that situations like this are proof of the old adage, "You cannot please ALL of the people ALL of the time." Coincidentally, years later when we were packing to move to another church, the same individual came to ask me to leave the drapes for they were "so right" for the house. This taught me to do the best I could and live with whatever came my way with happiness.

A family in the church decided to furnish one bedroom as a "Prophet's Chamber," a memorial to their family who were leaders in the church for decades. In keeping with their family traditions, they purchased the highest quality furniture and selected beautiful accessories. This was such a help in furnishing the home since we did not have four bedrooms of furniture. The room was beautiful and was used by many visiting preachers and missionaries. Certainly, it was a fitting memorial to this family.

One has to admire the devotion of church members who would be willing to get involved in something for which they get no personal benefit. I shall always believe that God rejoices when one of His children cares that much for His work, no matter what the involvement.

The furor did go away and life became normal. We were able to discern that this was not the ultimate home. We did find little things here and there, but they were minute compared to the epic undertaking. The church members were confident that we were in a veritable palace. I was truly glad when the newness wore off. Perhaps the greatest benefit to me was that of seeing what aspects of the home I truly loved and what I would like to have amended and in what way. When my turn to buy a home came along, I was fully equipped with my must haves, like to haves, and do not care for. God works mysteriously to teach us valuable lessons.

There was one resentment that did build up within me and which I prayed and worked hard to get over. We realized that we had the TOTAL responsibility for landscaping and sodding the spacious yards. That knowledge came when after several months in the house no move was made to accomplish the task. The result was a red muddy hill because the property had been scraped to make it level. So, there was no place for our child to play and hanging out clothes meant wading through mud! With NO experience in such things myself and with Charles away so much, I was expected to gather, on my own, the necessary items required to produce a showplace on that corner. One kind brother reminded me that I certainly did not want to detract from the beautiful house when I "fixed up" the yards. So, with a one year old toddler, I sprigged a 200 feet by 400 feet yard with Bermuda grass which I had dug and hauled. Mike and I would take his wagon every Friday afternoon and go up and down the streets of the town collecting the grass clippings where folks had edged their yards. This was free grass most of it with roots that I could take back and plant. Often we would go home and dump that wagon load and go off for another. We watered, fertilized, and protected the anticipated lawn. By the next summer, we had a beautiful thick lawn covering the whole area so green and inviting. On our forays with the wagon throughout the town, we were able to gather up cuttings for shrubbery and even some shrubs that had been discarded. The sum total was that we ultimately gained a yard that reflected the home.

Far and away, this is the hardest thing that I have ever done, physically. I still do not think that any deacon would have expected this of his wife. But, it fell my lot and I had the strength and tenacity to get it done. But it was difficult. On my knees in that sandy soil, I promised the Lord that if He would help me live through this, I would never do it again! I issued a warning to my husband that he need not expect it again. Imagine this—our next church built a home and I did another yard! So much for promising what you will and won't do. God in His infinite wisdom gave me more time on my knees. I was the winner.

Yes, after six years on that field, we were again involved with a Building Committee to build a new Pastor's home. There had been some work already done in the planning, location and ideas on finishing. The construction moved along quite efficiently and the home was done with far less complications. We moved from the six room, two bath home to a new ten room, three bath home with a huge, bare yard! By this time, I had learned to cope, knowing that this too would pass away. I enjoyed this experience and even endured the back breaking labor with a new joy and less resentment. I believe that the Lord just improved my attitude and gave me the physical strength to endure it all with happiness. How I do wish that I had been able to project that on the first project. In addition, by this time, we had three children, two of whom could help haul and plant grass. I loved that home and treasure its memory. Those yards were as pretty as the first ones and had roots of far greater benevolence from me. Ruth's attitude was a part of the reason.

Yet, this experience was not without difficulty. There were some snipes from disgruntled church members directed our way and Charles received full blame for the debt incurred, the changes, and it was called his house! I determined in my heart that preachers were not meant to be builders! The cost is high—yet inevitably worthwhile in the long run for the glory of God.

At a subsequent pastorate, early in our ministry there, a remark was casually made that a Pastor's home would be built eventually on a certain lot. My whole being came to full attention to help them find other ways to use their time, energy, and money.

An educational annex, even a sanctuary has the self-same effect, I have learned. All building programs are expensive spiritually. Unfortunately, divisions in a church can be wide and deep. The prevailing philosophy seems to be that the only way to heal a division is to change preachers. Of course, this is not true. The building still sits there and the notes are due at the bank in the same way. But, I suppose that is one way to clear the air and get a fresh start.

A Pastor friend remarked that the "best way to move from a church is to build a building." I disagree with this outlook, acknowledging the problems building gives a Pastor and his family; there are also many marvelous testimonies of God using buildings to His glory and improving the church program. Besides, turning the whole thing over to God will result in victory, not defeat. And that is a lesson well learned.

Conducting permanent Open House bothered me for many of our early years. Especially this has been true when we have had new homes. Every time someone in the community has company, they want to bring them to see the "new Pastor's home." When former members return to visit, the new home for the Pastor is certainly on their must see agenda. I grew accustomed to it over the years. One positive result of this is that I am a far better housekeeper than when I was first married or than my mother was. First thing out of bed in the morning, the bed is made! No dishes are left in the sink. Every effort is made to get the house into tip top shape before going to bed at night so that we are ready for early morning company.

When I was a very young bride, I had a visitor bright and early one morning. I was in the process of separating clothes to get the washer started when my visitor appeared. The bed was not made and breakfast dishes were still on the table and scattered over the kitchen. The paper from the night before was open on the floor of the living room and there were clothes scattered over the floor in the breakfast/laundry room. My visitor looked about with some surprise and informed me that she was there to "inspect the house" to see if I was keeping it well. Stunned? Well, yes! Her comment that my housekeeping might need some work because I was "so young" really hit home with me. She went into each room and even got on her knees to look under the bed. I had no idea that there would be "inspections." I thought that when I left home I was through having my room inspected. Not so! Looking heavenward as she lifted the dust ruffle of my bed, I prayed for forbearance, for patience, for anything! God must have heard, for I learned to truly love this lady and to be a much better homemaker.

I can guarantee one thing for sure and for certain: no one ever caught my house like that again! When my children got old enough to understand, they knew to keep their toys picked up and to make their beds when they first arose. I also learned to sort my colors and whites in a far more efficient manner. I suppose the adage, "Experience is the best teacher" still holds true.

Some years ago, we began to keep a Guest Book in the foyer of whatever home in which we were living. Many of our pop callers are surprised when we ask them to sign in. We have made some good friends and our church family has come to feel that their Pastor's home is their home. Now, I am able to look on this "presumption" with joy—most of the time. Knowing that our people identify so closely with us has been quite complimentary. Our children were reared to keep their rooms orderly and they were dismayed when visiting their friends to see "messy rooms." Sometimes, I think perhaps they missed a bit of freedom in their own wonderful home. I wondered at the effect this would have on them in their adult lives. I prayed for God's help to mold them properly. Now, they are adults and all three of them have their own homes where they do not pick up their clothes, nor remember to put the dishes away, nor tidy up before going to bed. I can only feel empathy for their spouses! I did try.

As our children grew, their needs changed and so did my responsibilities with them. When Mike started to school, the question of community involvement for me became a reality. I knew the importance of a good education and realized the value of knowing his school and being a part of it. So, I became a part of P. T. A. The now familiar pattern of demands placed upon Charles precluded him being actively involved, so the responsibility fell to me. I enjoyed the active involvement and readily accepted the office of treasurer for the next year. Working with the officers who were not from our church was a new found pleasure on which I thrived. The next year, I was elected president and this presented no problems in the church and allowed me to be a part of my child's educational process. Maintaining my church responsibilities was no problem and with the children getting older, my duties at home did not suffer. I felt that I was making a real contribution.

As the years have gone by, I have maintained my community activities. The extent of my involvement has varied from Pastorate to Pastorate dependent upon the opportunities available and the attitude of the local church congregation. The types of involvement have varied greatly. When our boys became old enough for scouting, I became a Cub Scout Den Mother, serving three years with Mike, plus four years with Mark. Then I spent one year as a Boy Scout Merit Badge counselor before becoming a brownie Girl Scout leader for our daughter, Charlaine. In addition, I served as Cheerleader Coordinator in support of the Little League Football program for three years spanning two different Pastorates.

From time to time, balancing my time effectively so that nothing suffered has been difficult. I have always tried to be involved in meaningful activities. If I saw no meaning, I did not become involved. I detest "busy work." Every community has needs from Scouting to sports, to politics. I never considered the latter, but found that my children were blessed by being involved with children from other churches in a social manner.

Many of my friends have shaken their heads at my attempts to be involved, but as the wife of a Pastor, I have found it a good way not only to be involved with my children but to meet people outside of our church. Yes, this has been a good way to invite people who are unchurched to find Christ as their Savior, to reach those seeking a church home, and to have a part in preparing today's youth for the responsibilities of tomorrow. After all, didn't Christ say, "Suffer the little children to come unto me" (Matthew 19:14 KJV)?

Our church people have shared my enthusiasm for the most part. Only once has it created problems and this was a unique situation. At the time, I was P. T. A. president for a public school where both of our boys were enrolled. This was the time of forced integration. The community in which we lived had studiously avoided integration even to the point of funding public education solely from local funds to avoid it. When the political situation compelled it, there were major problems. In spite of the low profile we had endeavored to maintain, there was indignation regarding my involvement and the fact that we would be sending our boys to an integrated school. Earnestly seeking God's leadership and knowing our financial situation, we sought to follow where He would have us go.

An excellent private school was established in the next town where many of our church families elected to send their children. In electing to send the boys to an integrated school, some Christians were alienated—they were sending their children who were my boys' friends to a school which was segregated. While we felt real compassion for them, we had to be fair with ourselves and our children. We could not afford to send our boys to a private school even if that had been our desire. In due time, things settled down and the integration went forward with no real problems. There was no way of avoiding the knowledge that some deep rifts in the community might never be healed. Fortunately, this was not the case in our church where the children all stayed friends regardless of where they went to school.

As a footnote, I might add that when we moved away, the next Pastor's wife was a public school teacher. The experiences we had already endured probably made it infinitely easier for her. You see, God does guide His Ruths and has a plan for every little thing.

All in all, our community involvement has been rewarding and our people have respected the efforts for the most part. I do believe that they really want a measure of this in their Pastor family, and it is good to be exposed to the entire community rather than to limit exposure only to one's own church. There is a thin line between too little and too much. Each Ruth must find her own niche and fill it.

Diversification was the hardest lesson to learn. When the children were very small, I was literally bound to home. I learned to look forward with great anticipation to Charles's coming home at night. The presence of an adult with whom to converse was a luxury. As he matured in his work and the demands grew, he was taken away from home more and more for meetings, revivals, appointments, counseling and just plain work. Increasingly, I found myself being both mother and father. The church demands placed upon us invariably increased during his absences. Often I lamented that he rarely left town without someone dying, becoming seriously ill, or experiencing a tragedy. Stepping into his shoes was expected and a Ruth will always try to fulfill these expectations.

At times, I have resented his travels, opportunities and positions. While I washed diapers and did his work, he flew off across the country to listen as great theologians preached and marvelous singers presented soul stirring music. He ate the best food and slept in beds he had not changed. I ate hamburgers and often did not sleep. He visited in the homes or our community while I supervised long division homework and prepared square meals. He presided over meetings while I sewed shirts and entertained the children of the neighborhood.

This green eyed monster called jealousy is poor company indeed with the power to overcome, devour and completely annihilate. If there is a way to totally conquer it, and dismiss it from life, I have not found it. My earnest prayer is still that one day God will give me the power of understanding all of this. Then, I would look at my children and realize that while I was not traveling and enjoying luxuries, I was overseeing the development of three little humans who will one day be a part of the leadership of tomorrow. Life does not get more important than that. Strange how God sees into the future and prepares us for it.

I still did not totally accept this role without some remorse. I felt that my children and I were being cheated of his presence too much. It was a long while before I accepted the situation and led my children to join me in making our time with Charles, what there was of it, the best of times. Without chafing at our situations too much, we learned to seize those times and enjoy them fully. Charles became the center of everything when he was at home. All too often he was like a guest in his own home when he was there. Yet, we knew that we could not ask him to stay at home and leave his work undone. His commitment would suffer and therefore, our relationship would lose its purpose. We learned to stay put and accept this way of life. Charles, in return, was deeply involved when he was at home. That is rich and rewarding involvement, albeit briefer than any of us would like. He managed discipline, sibling conflicts, counseling, and policy making when he was home. When he was not at home, I made the decisions which he did not overrule.

Revivals, Conventions, and Association business plus local church visiting, crises, daily ministering, and routine church meetings demand a great deal of any Pastor's time. There is no such thing as a "routine" or eight hour day. Rather, needs arise at any time and must be met, often immediately. Very early in our marriage, it became plain that God's church is always first, the family second. Not always has this been easy to accept as a part of Ruth's life. Instead, it can be miserable or happy. Personally, as a Ruth, I have tried to manage to find more satisfaction than sadness. Real doing has been required at times. However, I freely admit that ours is a special situation repeated in Pastors' homes throughout the world. This has occasioned and demanded humor, pathos, happiness, and grief in our varying situations. Not always has it been handled properly, but we do win more than we lose. One lesson that I have learned along the way is to realize that expecting anything at any given time is just the way one must live when meeting the needs of God's people.

I do remember when Michael was in the third grade and wanted to enter the Punt, Pass, and Kick Contest in our community. The first task that I had was to learn that means kick and throw a football in competition for distance and accuracy. Charles was totally inundated with Nominating, Finance, and deacon selection committees, plus his normal workload leaving NO time to help Michael. Coming from a family of all girls this was all foreign to me. What I knew about football would partially fill the eye of a needle with plenty of room left for the thread! But, this was my son and he wanted this so badly that I allowed him to register. He was given a book on *How to Punt, Pass and Kick* written by football professionals. My philosophy is that you can do anything if you first read the directions.

We read the book and began to practice. We worked, and I do mean we WORKED, each evening in our front yard. The entire neighborhood thought it was hilarious to see us laboring so intensively. We kept it up, learning how to use a tee—that is for holding the ball to kick, I learned—how to position the laces on the ball to properly pass (that means to throw). The day of the competition came and fathers were required to be with their sons. Charles was at home that Saturday morning, thankfully, but extremely reluctant to go with his novice son proclaiming that Michael knew nothing about how to perform in this competition. Finally, he was persuaded and took Michael off to the field. Imagine the scene in our home when Michael came home the third place winner! The word happiness is inadequate. See how God helps in even the most minute situations.

Not long after this, Mark decided to learn to ride a bicycle. Mark has never been as "devil may care" as Michael, so this was a real step forward for him. Again, we went to work. Each day while Michael was at school and Charlaine was napping, I would run behind that bike. Mark steered it into the flowers, a tree, a utility pole, the neighbor's house, and finally into the car! I decided that he would never ride alone and that I was doomed to run behind him—and just then, he balanced and off he went, smooth as silk. Panting and exhausted I just stared at him thanking God that He had given Mark a coordinated body after all. His dad was away preaching a revival and could not share this accomplishment, but we called him that night in order for him to lavish his son with praise while I hunted the liniment.

Charlaine decided to walk quite early in her life. We were not prepared for our seven month old to toddle. On the day she began to seriously pull up, I sensed something was about to happen and telephoned the church office asking Charles to come home for a while. Miracle of miracles, he was able to come and together we watched our baby take her first steps to her Daddy. For such a special moment, I was so grateful that he could share it.

You see, it is not easy for the Pastor either. He misses a great deal of joy. Also, he is not always available for emergencies. Mike had his tonsils out at age three, which was very traumatic for me. At that time, he was our only child. Imagine our total frustration when Charles was called away to a funeral in a distant town on the day of the surgery. Alone, I sent my child off to the cold operating room and alone I awaited the outcome. "I will lift up mine eyes unto the hills, from whence cometh my help. My help cometh from the Lord which made heaven and earth" (Psalm 121:1 KJV) took on a new meaning for me in that hour.

Then, there was the time that Charlaine developed a throat infection and went into convulsions while her daddy was two thousand miles away, attending a national convention. Again, the reassurance of the psalmist, "The Lord shall preserve thee. . ." (Psalm 121:7 KJV). So, while the Pastor misses joy, he misses responsibility also. This is not easy for him to hear. There is a measure of guilt that follows him regularly. Yet, ours is a mutual sharing relationship to the very best of our ability. When God empowers a man to minister, He also provides the tools and the outcome. Of that, I am certain.

By no means has ours ever been a normal life with family and personal pursuits. The demands are greater on all five of us than in the "normal" home. Yet, we did not elect this life; we were called into it by God Himself. So, the continual struggle is our way of life. Whether we count our experiences sacrifices or satisfactions is the clue to our happiness. In a very strange way, our children never seemed to really come to an awareness that life was a bit different for them. From their infancy, they more or less just rolled with it.

In building our life together, our goals have been almost always common. We agree on so many things—important and insignificant. Yet one of the saddest times of our life has been a Pastorate in which our joy was not in common. Charles was sublimely happy. He loved the town, the people in the church, the home, the geographical area, everything! I earnestly sought a single thing in which I might find joy. We went to that church under God's leadership—a joint venture. Soon thereafter, I realized that as much as I thought about being a Ruth, I was not truly dedicated. Why, I do not know until this day. I only know that times of differences are hard to endure. I taught an adult Sunday School class and worked with the youth, but the contentment that I had always enjoyed while being in the center of God's will just would not come to me regularly. Our marriage relationship suffered and our friendship for one another was altered briefly. Until God and I were able to resume our venture, Charles and I were almost strangers.

My church and community involvement did not suffer, I suffered. The church members never knew me as the Ruth I had promised to be and I shall always regret that. Be assured, my constant prayer is never to move that way again. Yet, homecoming was glorious when my spirit was conquered and my joy returned. My long, dark voyage to nowhere ended and I do believe that I cherish my role of Ruth more because of that interval. From it, I gleaned the ability to appreciate that and subsequent Pastorates with a new patience and to more thoroughly depend on God for directions and ". . . lean not to my understanding" (Prov. 31:5 KJV).

When our youngest child entered school, I took a job as an elementary reading aide—known as a paraprofessional. We realized that we had three children to send to college, one in only seven years. Knowing from our own experiences how expensive college was, we also knew that a Pastor's salary would not do that. I had not worked outside the home after seminary graduation until then—a period of fourteen years. But, we saw no other way. We knew that we could live on his salary and save all of mine and get a handle on college educations for them. I must admit, I went to work almost against my better judgment. The work of our church had grown tremendously and so much opportunity was there. I feared letting the people down, letting my family down, letting my husband down and most important, letting God down. I am an intensely emotional person, getting terribly involved in whatever I do. My strength, however, proved adequate for the occasion. I was overwhelmingly pleased with the way my careers merged. Home, school, church, not necessarily always in that order, came together and complimented one another beautifully. The fears I had harbored were never realized.

A career need not break up a home, nor interfere with the church. An outside career will not necessarily redirect one's thinking, thus making one a different person. The changes that I experienced were all for the good. I became more interesting to my children because I was in a school. I certainly understood them and their problems better than ever. Also, my relationship with my fellow teachers was good for me. They were not from our church and saw me not as "the preacher's wife," but as myself. I enjoyed that.

Our church people had mixed feelings about my job. They feared that I would abandon them and the work of our church. When they saw that I would not let the two conflict, they became very supportive. The compatibility of teaching and ministry, I am sure, contributed greatly to their attitude. We maintained our close affinity to the work of the church and the program increased. I was able to shoulder my portion of responsibility. My school responsibilities increased and when one area had to go lacking, I had a real problem.

My Name Is Ruth

Juggling the two became the secret art, and mastering it became my goal. I cannot say that I totally achieved it, but I can say that my life became more meaningful and I certainly made a larger contribution.

One Monday morning a little first grader came into my classroom with wide eyes proudly declaring, "I went to church yesterday and I saw you." Complimenting her, I inquired how she liked church. Grinning, she extolled the church bus, the Sunday school teacher, the refreshments, the stairs, concluding her narrative with, "I saw the preacher. He is Mr. Burgess. Do you know him?"

At school, I was Mrs. Burgess, the teacher. At church I was "the preacher's wife." At home I was still plain "Mama." Somehow God merged these identities. I could only remember, "In all thy ways acknowledge him and he shall direct thy paths (Prov. 3:6 KJV).

But, alas and alack, God's call came again, and Charles accepted a call to a church in the southern part of our state. This meant that our children would have to change schools: our oldest was in high school, the second in middle school, and the baby in elementary school. Each one was quite happy in their lives in that place with many friends and with happy plans to continue for many years. So, we had to explain to them how God had only good things in mind for them and that they would see how He would work things for their benefit since He loved them and wanted them to be happy and successful. Still, this was difficult for them to move in the middle of a school year.

Of course, the move prompted my resignation from the school and the joy that I had come to love. There was never a second thought. Calling upon my sincere reliance upon Ruth, I automatically accepted the "Whither thou goest. . ." (Ruth 1:16 KJV) and prepared for another move. Telling the church was difficult and convincing the children that this was going to be a great time in our lives and enumerating all of the way that things would change but still be the same, I was confident that we were, again, in the center of God's will.

The Road Not Taken

BY ROBERT FROST

Two roads diverged in a yellow wood,

And sorry I could not travel both

And be one traveler, long I stood

And looked down one as far as I could

To where it bent in the undergrowth;

Then took the other, as just as fair,

And having perhaps the better claim,

Because it was grassy and wanted wear;

Though as for that the passing there

Had worn them really about the same.

I shall be telling this with a sigh

Somewhere ages and ages hence:

Two roads diverged in a wood, and I—

I took the one less traveled by,

And that has made all the difference.

Chapter Six

A New Call

Serendipity is a lovely word meaning "a moment of great joy." Having been gifted with so many of those moments, I find it quite strange that one of my most memorable serendipitous experiences was particularly physically and mentally exacting to me. In fact, that serendipity set the tone for a time truly worthy of Ruth.

Leaving one church for another, we embarked upon a new experience. None of us knew what it would hold, least of all me. Prepared to accept a different house in a new geographical location where the children would be in new schools and we would be meeting all new people. Charles was confident that he was taking his family into a situation where all of us would be blessed and would be a blessing. We had to believe that God would not take us to anything less.

Of course, I was thinking about the job that I was leaving and wondering if there would be a situation awaiting me in this new place. I had enjoyed working with the students so much and participating in their learning was exciting. I was sad to be leaving, but in hopes that there would be a place for me in this new community. We had been able in my three years in the aide's job to determine that a teacher's aide salary does not provide enough income for three college educations despite all of our savings and hard work. This move would put us within commuting distance of a state university where the education program was not only award winning but highly regarded throughout the Southeast. While preparing to move, we discussed the possibilities of my working again, the approaching need to fund children in college, and what alternatives existed for us. After much prayer and consultation with trusted friends the decision was revealed to us from God himself. We saw that investing in my going to college and getting a degree to really TEACH would be worth it for our children's education. As a TEACHER rather than a Teacher's Aide, my income would be significantly increased— enough to put us in a position to be a bit more relaxed in handling the higher education of our children. Again, we leaned on the premise of spending money to make money. Having seen it work before, we were a bit braver this time.

At this time, I was a forty three year old woman who would be attending classes with eighteen year olds! Not a happy thought. But, this was our decision. I had a few credits from my night school twenty five years ago which, to my amazement, transferred. I drove to a nearby liberal arts college and took the College Level Entrance Program tests and to all of our surprise received enough credits to enter college as a junior. This program tests general knowledge and information from life experiences. Passing these tests saved two years of my time and no idea how much money. See what God can do?

Then came the old trial by fire, the entrance of Satan into our carefully laid plans. Just weeks into our ministry in this new church, I became quite ill. Pain and illness came together and exploded within my body. Each day I became worse by the hour. Here I was trying to settle into a new home, get my children adapted, learn the folkways and mores of a new group of people and a new church, and I was so very, very sick. Unwilling to admit my condition, I tried to keep on going. Finally, I realized that I needed help. Certainly, it was a providential act of God that our family physician at a former Pastorate had moved to a neighboring town. Having performed surgery on all three of our children, one of them twice, he was a trusted doctor and friend. Sitting in his office, ill and in great pain, I thought that I could handle anything if I could only feel good one more time. After a quick examination, he sent me off to the hospital for some tests and treatment. Briefly wondering what lay ahead for me, I was overcome with so much pain that I could only pray for relief at whatever cost.

Immediate tests indicated emergency major surgery. There was no way to avoid the experience and, I confess, that I anticipated relief with an emotion only call JOY! The relief did not come immediately, I had put off the surgery so long that I had to undergo several days of hydration and vitamins to build my system up to handle what was to come. I was totally unprepared for the reaction of our church members. We were so new on the field that I feared our church members would categorize me "sickly," a hypochondriac, or worse feel that we had not been honest in our dealings with them. Fleetingly, I considered asking for medication to help me cope for a few months at least to get things going. The doctor, a fine Christian man, assured me that my welfare was at stake and this was NOT acceptable. So, I entered the operating room with my pain and illness. Praying for a successful physical experience, I also prayed for our church relationship. Coming back from the never never land of anesthesia, I found my room filled, literally, with beautiful flowers, gifts, cards and notes. When visitors were allowed, our people came and wrapped me in a cocoon of loving concern from which I emerged physically sound and convinced that being a Ruth is the most marvelous experience that God can give to a woman.

Even now, I remember how unusual my meeting many of those church members was facilitated—

in my pajamas in a hospital room or in my pajamas in my bedroom at home as I recuperated.

This unorthodox experience of serendipity cemented a lovely Pastor People relationship and precipitated a more sincere dedication on my part. From the painful beginning of this Pastorate, we moved right into the mainstream of a meaningful ministry because we had moved into the lives of our people. They knew that we were human. We knew that they cared. Oh, that this experience could be repeated in the home of every Ruth. Serendipity.

After I was thinking more or less clearly, I began to remember the plan for me to go to school. What difference would all of this health business make? We did what every Christian does; we took it to the Lord in prayer. I was doing well, was back to teaching my Sunday school class and beginning to work with the youth. Home was settling down as the children accepted that they were here to stay, and our church seemed to be where God wanted us to be. The revelation came: this location had been planned by the One who knows all. I was close enough to make the round trip commute to college every day, had a car that would make the trip with no trouble, I had been admitted, my classes were set up and I even had a scholarship to pay the way. "GO!" God seemed to be saying.

So, I did. True, the students with whom I sat in class could easily have been my own children! In fact, on the first day of the term, I walked into one classroom, and as I looked around to determine where I wanted to sit, one of the students said, "Professor, do we have to have our book today?" I looked behind me and realized, this kid thought that I was the teacher!!!! That experience happened many other times during my time in college.

After two years of overloading and going to school year round, I walked the aisle to receive by Bachelor's degree in English Education with my own cheering section—my children and my husband. I drove the seventy mile round trip every day, missed only one day of class, and graduated *summa cum* laude. In a fit of irony, I did my Student Teaching in the very high school where my oldest son was a high school senior. He assured me that he did not mind!

During the last quarter of classes, we were required to attend a Career Fair and interview with at least two schools for a job. All of the schools from nearby counties as well as the major systems in the State of Georgia were there. As I did my interviews, I could tell that they were surprised that I was not twenty one years old, but no one said it outright. Wonder of wonders, the first interview that I had was with a neighboring system where I was called back for another interview and they hired me. I was to begin actual TEACHING within two weeks. So, I got my first teaching job and began the road to financial ability to educate the children.

But, there was far, far more to it than that. For the decades of our marriage, I had been following in Charles's steps, standing at his side, answering what I felt to be God's calling for my life. These had been rewarding times for me, and I was comfortable. With my degree in my hand and a job handed to me, a new awareness came over me. God's call to me had expanded—not changed, just expanded. I was still a Pastor's wife, a mother, a Sunday school teacher, a Girls' Auxiliary leader, a youth worker—NONE of that had changed. There were still groceries to be bought, meals to be cooked, homework lessons to be supervised, floors to clean, and all of the other tasks that go with being a homemaker. But, I was also the Pastor's wife and a church member. Now, I was given the opportunity to move out of my comfort zone—physically and mentally—into a whole new area. I remembered the Great Commission, "Go ye therefore and teach all nations...." (Matthew 28:19). Could this be the mission call that I had answered so long ago when I was only sixteen years old? I had wanted to go to Africa and build buildings where students would learn to read. Instead, I would go into a classroom and teach teen agers to compose and write and to understand literature building learning that would facilitate their lives. What a challenge! Did God expect too much of me? Could I measure up?

Yes, my call expanded. The first day that I walked into my classroom as a teacher, I stood there all by myself for a bit, looked around at the empty desks, the chalkboards, the books, and prayed that God would make me worthy of the task. Like I had done when we were planning to be married, I turned it all over to God and trusted Him for the outcome. I will admit that on the first day of school when the students joined me in that classroom, I had to pray long and hard again. God had given me a new career to go with the former one and this one was to be totally different. He and I were in it together.

In those first years, as I carried out my responsibilities and settled into this new role, I NEVER for one moment comprehended the master plan that God was carrying out in my life. My goal was simple: stay in the center of God's will and trust Him for the results. I just wanted my children to be able to go to college. Little did I know, nor could I have imagined what fruit all of this would yield for my children or for me. Yet, God was at work from the beginning, just as He has always promised.

Our life as a married couple has been built within the will of God. The nebulous threads of love, compassion, friendship and understanding, all given and received, have woven a beautiful tapestry, embroidered with patience, maturity and total dependence upon God. This has been enough with which to build a life. All that it has taken is to remember with each sunrise that "Thy God shall be my God" (Ruth 1:17)

Hymn, "So Send I You"

So send I you to labour unrewarded
To serve unpaid, unloved, unsought, unknown
To bear rebuke, to suffer scorn and scoffing
So send I you to toil for Me alone

So send I you to bind the bruised and broken
Over wandering souls to work, to weep, to wake
To bear the burdens of a world a weary
So send I you to suffer for My sake

So send I you to loneliness and longing
With hart a hungering for the loved and known
Forsaking kin and kindred, friend and dear one
So send I you to know My love alone

So send I you to leave your life's ambition
To die to dear desire, self will resign
To labor long, and love where men revile you
So send I you to lose your life in Mine

So send I you to hearts made hard by hatred
To eyes made blind because they will not see
To spend, though it be blood to spend and spare not
So send I you to taste of Calvary

"As the Father hath sent me, so send I you"

-       Margaret Clarkson, 1915.

162

Chapter Seven

On Disappointments

Years ago as the happy bride of a minister, I looked forward to a future filled with useful service to our Lord in a partnership of love. As the years rolled by, I learned that all of this was not only possible but wonderful. The words of Margaret Clarkson's beautiful hymn, "So Send I You," became a sort of inspiration for us. It was an energizer when we were low and a praise when we were high.

As our children arrived, we found solace in "So send I you to loneliness and longing, with heart a hungering for the loved and known. . ." You see, each of our children arrived hundreds of miles from grandparents, aunts, and uncles. Still unswerving and relentless, we went on ". . . to bind the bruised and broken, o'er wandering souls to work, to weep, to wake."

Then, after years of ". . . leaving life's ambition and dying to dear desire and self-will. . ," of service and labor, we came up against a new obstacle. We found it insurmountable, overwhelming, a veritable bulwark of unreasonable dimensions.

A group of deacons on a mission they deemed necessary came to say that they felt Charles's ministry was over! As I heard the words, I remembered, "So send I you to labor unrewarded, to serve unpaid, unloved, unsought, unknown. . ." These men made no charge, they had no grievance, ". . . to bear rebuke, to suffer scorn and scoffing. . ." They intimated that they could sway the church to vote us out—"So send I you to hearts made hard by hatred, to eyes made blind because they will not see. . ." As I listened to these men, almost in a trance, I looked at this man who had given so much, and who was now being humiliated. I heard a sound, a clinking and I wondered?

Then I heard my husband speak of God's call, God's leadership, God's love, *God's* church and his determination to follow God *even now*, ". . .to spend tho' it be blood—to spend and spare not— so send I you. . ." It was with humble pride that I looked anew at this man with whom I had shared so much and realized, as perhaps never before, he WAS God's man! No Board of Deacons, no gossip mongers, no critical women could sway his call of commitment.

As those men filed out of our living room, promising to oust their Pastor—my husband—the strange clinking sound came again and suddenly I knew what it was. Either it was the rattling of thirty pieces of silver or the shaking of dice for the coat of the Master.

You see, the weak are still with us. They bear different countenances. Some are deacons, some are women who love to talk, some are temptresses, some are jealous, and some are power hungry, unsaved church members. Yet, the weak are still with us. . ."So send I you—to taste of Calvary. As the Father hath sent me, so send I you."
Every Pastor's ministry is subjected to periods of tempest, turmoil, rebuke, questioning and unrest. Ours was no exception. I know that these were the times for which I certainly was unprepared. In my heart, doing God's will was the most exciting, important and fulfilling life possible. I simply could not imagine the prying inquisitions, factions, unrest and tempest that I learned existed in the church.

I was so naïve—although this is an inadequate description—to believe that God's people would always live up to the standards He set for the church. Yet, I did believe! I trusted that all Christians held their church in high esteem, viewing its work with awe. There are simply no words to convey the terrible disappointment—the letdown—the shock—the emptiness—the utter dismay—the total desolation that I experienced upon discovering that God's church people, some of them at least, have "feet of clay."

That occasion has all but faded. The results are indelible.   It was a minor episode in the beginning that snowballed into a veritable avalanche.   The specifics vary; however, the reality is the same—power.

The church of the twenty first century still seeks to weaken God's power. Part of the reason is fear, jealousy, ignorance and the never failing influence of Satan. The first church felt these influences and Luke recorded some of them in The Acts of the Apostles, chapter four. This was "The Council." Mere mortals were they who sought to put down God and His power by putting down God's man.

They asked each other, "What shall we do with these men? . . . We can't deny that they have done a tremendous miracle, and everybody knows about it . . . But perhaps we can stop them from spreading their propaganda. We'll tell them that if they do it again we'll really throw the book at them" (Acts 4:16 thru 18 TLB). Two thousand years later, the same thing happens.

Ridiculous you say, no one has such feelings today. But they do all of this and more IN God's church under the guise of Christianity, under the name of "church member." Their name is Legion . . .disgruntled deacons who want things "the way that they used to be"—who needs

progress?. . .deposed leaders who no longer find
themselves on the center stage, sought for
counsel and decisions. . .women who connive to
gain the attention of God's servant in infatuation
akin to "puppy love" and the clique who
heretofore had its hold on everything and is
dispersed into organization to reach out. . .the
"old members" who resent the newcomers, new
members brought into God's kingdom. . .the
gossipers who LOVE to talk about everything
true or false.

Not so ridiculous is it? Each church has them—
every one! The question is how much power do
they have in God's church today? Too often the
answer is too much power. Have you heard of
the church across the way which "ran the
preacher off. . .or the preacher's wife whose
reaction to all the critics, criticism and
condemnation drove her to a nervous breakdown.
. .the church that split because some wanted to
grow and others did not. . .the Pastor who
resigned and went into secular work because of
the continual harassment. . .and on and on. . .the
gossip mongers are busy and successful. Their
work is done well, with no real purpose, nothing
except the reigning power of the same Satan who
ruled "The Council" in Acts chapter four.

This sounds so sad, so hopeless. Luke said in
Acts 4:26 (TLB) "The kings of earth unite to
fight against him, and against the anointed Son of

God!" Yes, it is happening all around us today. The newsletter of a Ministers' Wives group estimates 73 percent of the wives of full time ministers are on tranquilizers, citing pressure and criticism, demands and inability to "fight back." Forty thousand ordained ministers have left the ministry in less than ten years, cites a counseling firm. Why? Mr. and Mrs. Church Member are often the reason! Those who fit the categories of agitator, gossiper, lack of interest, antagonist, power hungry, lack of dedication and inability to heed Christ's command, "Go ye."

But, they are not alone. Mr. and Mrs. Church Member who sit by idly and let it all happen are also guilty. That command of Christ goes further. . . "Lo, I am with YOU always" (Acts 1:8 KJV).

There are no statistics on harassing phone calls, visits by "well-meaning Christians" who deem "your work has ended." Oh, God calls you and your family here, blesses and guides your work, but it is sometimes the semi faithful church member who decides it is over. No one knows the heartache that goes with teaching a Sunday school class when members walk out. There is no measure for ridicule and verbal abuse. No one to whom it has not happened can know the deep thud of the words, "We want you out, so we can get someone else."

You see, Acts chapter four goes further. Those thus persecuted prayed, "O Lord hear their threats, and grant to your servant boldness. . .After this prayer, the building shook and they were filled with the Holy Spirit and boldly preached God's message. All the believers were of one heart . . . and there was warm fellowship among all believers" (Acts 4:31). TLB).

So, thank God, there are stalwarts who take their Christian responsibility seriously, who pray and who stand up and are counted. There are those who look beyond today and toward tomorrow, and even beyond. There are those who count the cost and find eternity with God infinitely more valuable than momentary service of the devil for the sake of popularity or going with the "others". Thank God!

There is hope.

If God's people rise up and stand for that in which they believe; if they read their Bibles, pray, worship and give obedience to God, then we will have a Pentecost . . . a revival . . . a return to the mission of the church.

And, after all, we DO all have claim to the promise, "Lo, I am with you always" (Acts 1:8 KJV) and the great promise, "My God shall supply all you need according to his riches in glory by Christ Jesus" (Phil. 4:19 KJV).

So, how do we lend strength to God's church? We preach, we pray, we witness, we educate, and we win others! In the face of criticism, censure, no cooperation, and all efforts to weaken the witness, we who are God's people keep on keeping on. For, we are called to overcome with the words of Jesus Christ, "You shall be my witness" (Acts 1:8 KJV) and we have answered, "Here am I Lord, use me." Nobody said it would be easy—Calvary was not easy. No one demands success—only faithfulness. . . "And yet shall receive power after that the Holy Ghost is come upon you" (Acts 1:8 KJV).

Power—the power to endure, to stand tall and to be able, on judgment day to hear Him say, "Well done thou good and faithful servant" (Matthew 25:23 KJV)—and that makes it all worthwhile—not easy—but worth remembering.

"Blessed are ye, when men shall revile you, and persecute you, and shall say all manner of evil against you falsely, for my sake. Rejoice and be exceeding glad; for great is your reward in heaven; for so persecuted they the prophets which were before you."

Matthew 5:11 thru 12 KJV

WHAT DO YOU DO?

What do you do when you've done your best?

But somehow you know you have failed the test,

And your hope is as sere as last year's leaf?

When you're left alone to examine your grief?

What do you do when there's no more to say?

I'll tell you what—you kneel and pray!

Patricia Sutton

1954

Chapter Seven

Other Disappointments

When one is engaged in doing God's work and feels so confidently to be in the center of God's will, only good things can happen. Right? No indeed. Remember the story of Job? God used that man and those times to accomplish some timeless lessons for those of us who would follow. Hard times and disappointments, after all, are a part of life. When one surrenders a life to God's work, then that has to include disappointments as well. Some of these surpass disappointments and become heart rending experiences. Thank goodness those are in the minority. Disappointments, however, have become a part of our ministry from time to time. The important thing to remember is that overcoming them is God's promise and He is always there.

One such incident came in our lives. All disappointments are not made by others. We make some of our own. Our experience was of an entirely different nature. A woman in our church felt strongly attracted to my husband. I had read and heard that this was not unusual. Seems that many women fantasize themselves in love with their minister or physician, calculating the attentiveness of ministering to be personal, physical affection. This particular woman had a personal problem some of which she shared with me. Due to the nature of her situation, I am positive there were larger problems, counsel for which she sought my husband. She was a church leader, a fairly attractive woman and well known in the community. I was aware of a growing attachment on her part and brought it to my husband's attention. Perhaps the foundation for my feeling was jealousy, I do not really know. I loved him. Further, I believed in him. He was my Pastor, a spiritual leader and I expect him to keep the commitment stated in I Timothy chapter three. When the little warning lights went off in my brain, I shared them with him.

We are not a demonstrative couple. Ours is a "sane and sensible" marriage. We love each other, but our love transcends the physical. When God brought us together and called us to His service, He gifted us with a capacity to find fulfillment in each other that is satisfying, even if it is not the skyrocket romantic love of magazines. In the bloom of our life together, there was not time nor energy to concentrate on a flirtatious physical relationship. The best of ourselves has always been channeled into our work. Looking back, I wonder if this was altogether good. I challenge the wisdom of failing to enjoy one another fully in our youth. I believe that our unity of purpose is total, and our relationship is deeply fulfilling; however, I cannot help but believe we may have missed out on a bit of the joy of building that relationship.

At any rate, this woman developed a feeling for him that led me to great heartache and desolation. In her mind, she imagined him to be as unhappy in his life as she was in hers. She saw herself able to meet the needs that she thought I could (or would) not meet. As I sought to alternately ignore, detour and expose this situation, I became her friend. Ironic though it may seem, I found myself listening to her extol my husband's virtues, and her feelings for him. Totally confused, I sought to counsel, chastise, and startle her. I believe, honestly, that I tried everything except to play the part of the neglected or betrayed little wife. Finally, one day, she brought me up short by stating flat out, "You know, I always get friendly with the wife of every man with whom I have an affair!"

I was aghast! Words and actions failed me. Stunned, I confronted my husband. He was apathetic, accusing me of jealousy and making mountains out of molehills. We wound up arguing with raised voices, reminders, warning, and all of the terribly immature and unfair arguments rolled out and into an avalanche of tears and anger. Unfeeling, he stood on his statement that all of this was in my head and that I should not do this to him much less to myself.

Still believing, or wanting to believe, in him, I tried to put it behind me. It did not work. Instead, I began to do a bit of imagining myself. The so called "affair" became very real to me. It was horrible. But, the mind is strong. Our marriage suffered traumatically. Not only the communications broke down, so did everything else. For the very first time, I wondered, even imagined life without Charles outside the church. She was able to hold her head high and go on with her life while my heart broke into tiny pieces.

The episode lasted, all told, about three months from onset until we came to grips with it. The effects of it were far more lasting.

Recovery was not easy. Having experienced doubt, it became easier to be suspicious of every woman who called or came to our home or his office. I was miserable, so was everyone else. Charles and I were not happy together. Overcoming this experience came with remembering the forgiveness that was mine through Jesus Christ. If He could forgive so much, why could I not do the same? Realizing this made my salvation more precious and enabled me to overcome my fears. Really, I grew marvelously, but the price was high. I am so grateful that I have never had to cope with a real affair; the imagined one almost did me in. Yet, even today, I know that there are conniving unhappy women who must exercise their fantasies. I try very hard to sympathize. Charles, I believe, also learned a valuable lesson. (Not the least of which was to pay attention when I tell him something!) At any rate, that particular disappointment has not been repeated.

So, disappointments come in all kinds of ways. Some Pastors' wives are really exceptional in the way that they handle these disappointing intervals. Others retreat into themselves, wallowing in self-pity. Unknowingly, by so doing, they literally join the opposition forces. Still others back away, like a burned child, and are never able to return to the total fellowship. You see, there really exists between God and Ruth a very special relationship of total communication. The fragility of this unique union is easily spoiled by the turmoil of the Pastoral teapot tempests. Yet the stability of this same union can be strengthened by the selfsame experience. The difference is how the problem is handled.

One can be quite exceptional in the way she handles such intervals. The primary requirement is that it be made quite clear that one's loyalty is to God first, then to her husband; yet, at the same time, she must remain unchanged and warm toward all of those who might be antagonistic. I learned that my smile and concern must be genuine and that I must cultivate the unique ability to understand people without compromising my own principles. I am sure that I have benefited from this premise and I like to think that situations have been stabilized and brought into true focus.

During a particularly tumultuous Pastoral situation, my husband was totally immersed in an unbelievable situation. Suddenly, it seemed that God had forsaken him. He felt so betrayed that he was ready to leave the Pastoral ministry. There had been a disagreement among some of the older families of the church and sides had been chosen throughout the church. Feelings were hurt; bad blood was revealed; emotions were running wild and everything in the church become involved—every department, every ministry, every activity. Suspicions were rampant. Rumor spread throughout the community as sides were chosen. There was no way that God was being honored and ministries met.

The day that he came home and announced that he was going to resign, I was stunned beyond belief. We had three children, two dogs, a cat, nine rooms of furniture, a large trampoline, three bicycles, two cars and an attic full of keepsakes in a house owned by the church from which he was resigning. We had no house of our own into which we could move, and our small savings were totally inadequate to begin a new life. Certainly, all of these physical things flooded my consciousness. Yet to my bewildered soul, a peace arose that shouted, "God will take care of you." Never shall I forget that time. I was at the washer on a cold weekday morning when Charles came in to make the announcement that he was going to resign. Cold chills shook my being as we moved into the seldom used living room to discuss our situation. God's will, a future (?), and yes, what had brought us to this place. In retrospect, I wonder that I did not scream, cry or lash out. I truly believe that God had conditioned me for this moment without my awareness. My philosophy took words:

A man must do what he must do. And a woman must do what she must do as well. What must be done must be done, no matter what agony it entails. Only when we have earned the privilege of finding a sanctuary in one another can we find God's solace, and thus go on even through the dark hours. We faced up to the fact that the time had come and might even come again, when we must go out and face it all!

This experience lasted for eight weeks. I believed there was a Pastoral future and was unable to lock it out nor contemplate seeking a secular life. He covered all avenues of possibility as he completed the Pastoral tasks involved in his resignation notice. We looked at newspaper want ads and sought out employment listing agencies. Our home stayed intact by some miracle of God. The church people were divided—those who sought to spiritually support us and those who stood back to see what would happen.

Serenity in the midst of a volcano made this a beautiful experience. That serenity was the assurance of God's leadership. On one particularly sleepless night, I found the words and told my husband, "I can cope with anything, but if we run from this thing it will come pounding after us no matter where we try to hide." Now, this was unique in that it came from me. Charles's philosophy has always been that one cannot run away from any situation. So it was on that night that we agreed that should we leave God's leadership, all we had discovered therein would turn sour. We could not afford to be bitter lest our lives of service turn violently against us. How long would we be able to pretend outside God's leadership? A year, two, three? Sooner or later the disobedience would overtake us and we would have squandered the ability to fight it. What then?

A silence so wide, deep, and complete it could be felt engulfed us both. After a time, I said, "This would mean watching you die in little pieces." Suddenly, we were on our knees side by side. What his prayer was, I do not know. There were no audible words. With God, I reviewed our lives and concluded with a plea for a sign as to what road we should take. I reminded God, who already knew, that we had only four weeks left of our allotted time in this house. I assured Him of my belief that "All things work together for good," (Romans 8:28 KJV) and my commitment to "Arise and shine" (Acts 1:8 KJV).

Dawn came. Exhausted, I went off to take the children to school. Wearily, I dragged home physically drained, emotionally spent, spiritually numb, and trembling. That night, after a nondescript dinner, I sat down with my Bible while Charles went to visit in the hospital. (Ironically, the man whom he was visiting was the instigator of the current church problem and now gravely ill.) The phone rang. I spoke with a pulpit committee chairman in a town of which I had never heard regarding a church I never knew existed. Eight weeks later, we moved our family to that town and into that church's Pastor's home where Charles would be the Pastor of that church.

"Blessed are ye, when men shall revile you, and shall persecute you falsely for my sake. Rejoice and be exceedingly glad for great is your reward in heaven for so persecuted they the prophets which were before you" (Matt 5:11 thru 12 KJV). Only the reward does not always wait until heaven!

180

I did not see my husband so torn again. Our lives reached a new zenith and this was the happiest and most successful Pastorate. He bloomed, his service was exemplary and his commitment total.

That church which was so divided split into the two groups. After some time had gone by, one of the subsequent churches failed, but those members did not return to their former church. Information coming to us indicated that many of them gave up on church. You see, when man takes over running God's work, there can be no real progress. God has to be in it. When He is not, problems arise.

God works in strange ways . . . but he does work—it we allow him. Ruths know this instinctively. "Thy God shall be my God. . ." (Ruth 1:16 KJV).

SLOW ME DOWN, LORD

Ease the pounding heart by the quieting of my
mind,
Steady my hurried pace with a vision of the
eternal reach of time.
Give me, amid the confusion of the day, the
calmness of the everlasting hills.
Break the tensions of my nerves and muscles
with the soothing music of singing
Streams that live in my memory.
Help me to know the magical, restoring power of
sleep,
Teach me the art of taking minute vacations—of
slowing down to look at a flower, to chat with a
friend, to pat a dog, to read a few lines from a
good book.
Slow me down, Lord, and inspire me to send my
roots deep into the soul of life's enduring values
that I may grow toward the stars of my greater
destiny.
-        Author Unknown

". . . my cup runneth over" Psalm 23:5 KJV

Chapter Eight

Mountaintops

Biblical personalities continually express their joy or great happiness by stating "Hallelujah." In my mind this is a shout of victory, a prayer of thanksgiving, and more importantly, an expression of great joy! I found this acclamation totally acceptable to provide the proclamation of mountaintop experiences. These times of great joy often defy description. Perhaps the best way to communicate the beauty of a mountaintop experience is to recount, mentally, the valleys. Having experienced loneliness, fatigue, unhappiness and frustration and then suddenly break out of the darkness into the glorious sunlight of contentment, excitement, satisfaction, peace and thanksgiving is like ascending to the mountaintop and surveying all that has been, is and will be from the confident shelter of God's guiding hand.

When we were living in New Orleans, we would drive to Georgia to visit our families occasionally. The drive back to New Orleans was always long and tedious, I suppose because we were leaving those who loved us and going back to the everyday grind. I would be so weary of being inside the car for so long; but, then we would approach Mobile, Alabama. On old U. S. Route 90 there is a steep curve in the road and when coming out of it, there spread out before the eyes was Mobile Bay in all of its glory. There would be sunbeams bouncing off of the water, sailboats making white dots here and there, and far on the horizon, a ship making its way into port with goods from somewhere exotic. The rich green of vegetation and trees at the water's edge, cliffs verdant with nature's green were outstanding. Each time, I beheld that scene, my fatigue disappeared as if God had given me a glimpse of my tomorrows and they were beautiful even with responsibility on the horizon. That will always stand as one of the greatest mountaintops in my life, even though it was really the Gulf of Mexico. I got perspective and gave thanks. God uses many instruments to assuage our doubts, fears, fatigue and to give us hope, reason, and courage. I never came away from that view without being reinvigorated and totally at peace. Hallelujah!

At times, my mountaintops are small insignificant events, meaningless except to me. For instance, a Ruth finds fulfillment and release in being in a total relationship with her husband. So little time is available for togetherness that moments become mountaintops.

At other times, it would seem that we would get all involved with one of our discussions. We were both great talkers. Charles spoke at many civic and religious meetings in addition to his regular preaching and speaking responsibilities in the church. I taught classes in the church regularly in addition to my teaching job. Yet the privilege of talking to just one person is special. So much of the conversation with friends is limited to running into someone in a public place, or rushing through a dinner to get to a meeting. We would sit and talk sometimes through the night and be absolutely astonished to see daylight come. When your mate is also your best friend, there is the entire world in the room when you are together. That is how it was with just the two of us. Hallelujah!

Other mountaintop experiences which have provoked supreme happiness are more tangible. The day Charles was ordained was a spiritual peak. The presence of God was so real that it was transcending. Truly, it was a setting apart. Whenever times are difficult spiritually, the recall of that moment of total public surrender insures an instant mountaintop! Perhaps there are those who feel ordination to the gospel ministry is for the man only. I definitely was a part of Charles's ordination and felt then and now the power of the Holy Spirit and the knowledge of being in the center of God's will. Hallelujah!

Perhaps the sweetest mountaintop experience is that supremely satisfying knowledge that comes from being in the palm of God's hand. Scoffers quickly dismiss this intangible as being impossible. Since I was sixteen years old, I have known the reality of this unique experience. At that time, I answered God's call to commit my life to His service. Having known, at that time, the sheer joy of total surrender, I have never been able to understand why everyone does not diligently seek God's will for their lives. Giving over the control of one's life to the power of God's spirit evokes satisfaction. Following His will leads to mountaintops. Hallelujah!

We have lived physically in many locations. People constantly ask where we would rather be. Absolutely no thought is required to reply "in the center of God's will." Therein is security, happiness, satisfaction, and fulfillment. The most overwhelming joy about this location is the joy of making a contribution. Hallelujah!

A most pleasant mountaintop is the continued acceptance I have experienced as a Ruth. Feeling a part of a church family when being acknowledged as their Pastor's wife is extraordinarily sweet. Infinitely sweeter is to feel their acceptance of me for myself, in addition to the role in which I am cast. I suppose this experience is made more joyful because I am so aware of God's hand in my life. Hallelujah!

The awareness that I am regularly growing in my every relationship is particularly rewarding. I can think of no greater sadness than being stagnant. The wisdom with which God gifts His children is sufficient to enrich every niche of my life. Life's every experience becomes fascinating and important. Our marriage relationship, my spiritual relationship, indeed every facet of life is constantly maturing. Certainly, this is a joy worth much thanksgiving.

Counting one's blessings is always a humbling experience. This activity makes one aware of how much God really does. Even more difficult is putting one's blessings in priority order. Transcending difficult, this task borders the impossible. This is true of putting my mountaintops in order of importance. They are all of infinite value in my life; however, if not my pinnacle, very close to the top of my list of joys is the blessing of our children.

One question most magazine marriage suitability tests include is, "If you cannot have children, will you consider adoption?" The "yes" that we so quickly answered before we married would have a profound effect on our lives. We both wanted children. Had we not, marriage would not have been nearly so important.

We married, years passed and still we were childless. We began to wonder if something was wrong. Finally, while completing the Seminary, we decided to satisfy the empty gnawing within us that kept us uneasy. Why no family after five years of marriage?

A nurse friend confided that a childhood accident in which Charles had been electrocuted with 19,000 volts of electricity might be our problem. Taking the initiative, he saw a doctor who pronounced him "iffy," recommending a gynecologist for me. Without hesitation, we made the first of what would be many visits. I began my treatment for endometriosis and perhaps infertility—a word that still sounds empty and incomplete.

For years everything possible was done to help us conceive. Nothing worked, but we always had hope. "Next time it will work." Finally, the doctor gently suggested that we consider adoption, citing cases of patients who had successfully adopted children. As I sat listening to his kind words, and observed all of his efforts to be helpful, one thought pounded at my heart. I had to tell Charles. Numbly, I drove across the metropolitan city of New Orleans to the apartment we had so hoped would be home for our child. My world seemed to have stopped. Traffic was at its peak, but I was never so alone.

I felt like an empty shell and cried out, "Why us?" I was driving along a four lane highway near what is now the Super Dome where the New Orleans Saints play football, when I got an answer. God was in that car with me. He spoke to me just as surely as can be, when He said, "Have faith. Do not give up. I am in this with you."

Although still shaken, I saw the beginning of a ray of light or hope.

That night, we faced the truth. Likely, we would never have a child. Without saying it in so many words, we concluded that we must adopt! A long chapter in our lives began. We sought adoption agencies, investigated requirements and immediately learned that as long as I must work, we were not eligible for consideration. Since Charles was still in school, I had to work; however, graduation was not too far away.

There was in New Orleans at that time, a Baptist "Home for Unwed Mothers and Adoption Center." I volunteered to help there. In so doing, my entire life underwent a great change as I saw girls from all walks of life come there. Some came alone, some with their families, some with a boyfriend, but they all came to have a baby knowing that it would be adopted to another family, that they would most likely never see it. They were also assured of the best of medical care and counseling along with the knowledge that the family selected for their child would have been vetted and the perfect choice.

I helped some of them with homework, listened to some of them weep, some were angry and railed at their parents or boyfriend for not standing by them. Many of them were indifferent just wanting the experience to end. A part of my volunteering was to visit the hospital when a girl had given birth. The home sent a dozen red roses, and a visit was assured in the effort to present to the other mothers that this one was no different. This was vital for her self-esteem. These visits were often sad as the girl was now faced with the fact that she would not see this child; but there was joy in that the experience was over and that a family somewhere was going to be so blest. This did so much to prepare me for the experiences ahead.

Relieved of some of the burden of realizing that we would not have a biological child, I did see more doctors to assure my own health. We finished out our time in New Orleans with the knowledge that armed with his degree; Charles would be led by God to a church quite soon. We depended upon God to lead us to a Pastorate, so we waited. By now, waiting was the theme of our lives. One month before his graduation, Charles received a request from a church in Georgia to meet with their Pulpit Committee while we were home for Christmas. So, a day after Christmas we met with the Committee. They talked to both of us for a bit and then asked to speak with Charles alone. While I read a book and waited, they talked about important things, the culmination of which was they invited him to preach at the church before we went back to Louisiana. God was at work, we were confident. Still we prayed sincerely for His guidance in the matter. Deciding to leave from the church after the Sunday night service and drive back to New Orleans, we packed our car and said goodbye to our families and embarked on a brand new road.

We spent the day with such wonderful people in a very nice little town with some amazing people. What a blessing it was! Then we drove all night to get back so that we could get on with our responsibilities. Arriving at our apartment early on that Monday morning ready to fall into bed and sleep, our neighbor banged on our door to tell us that he had tickets for us to the Sugar Bowl football game! Charles NEVER turned down a football game. So, with no sleep, we took off for Tulane Stadium and the game. The next Sunday, the church issued a call and we looked at each other aware that I would not have to work in this new place and we could go on with our adoption plans. We moved to that church field. This became our new home.

Upon hearing of our childless plight, a local doctor suggested an endocrinologist nearby, assuring us that if he could not help us no agency would turn us down. So we began again all of the tests and treatments along with the hoping and the waiting. At length, he too finally recommended adoption.

At our local Family and Children's Service, we began to fill out the seemingly endless forms, and began a new kind of waiting. We furnished medical reports, references, had our home inspected more than once, reported our financial situation, and duly recorded the physical statistics of our entire family on both sides. After eight months of intensive formalities, we were accepted for child placement and quietly prepared a nursery while waiting.

Nine months later, as we were having lunch, our social worker telephoned. From Charles's voice, I knew this was it. The state had found us a baby—a boy, six months old! We were to visit him, and if we liked him and he liked us, he was ours. Words cannot express my feelings. I burned the pecan pies I was baking for our church supper. Neither of us could concentrate; we were about to be parents, but could tell no one. We shopped for clothing in a nearby town, now that we knew a child was imminent. Not knowing what size to buy, we bought several sizes, spreading them out on the guest room bed so that we could just look at them. We were both in awe. We purchased a bed, a playpen and dozens of diapers. A small room at the front of the house was designated the nursery and we filled it with what we thought that we needed.

Time came for the visit and we were so afraid. We both had visions of the beautiful child (we knew that he was beautiful, automatically) bursting into tears at the sight of us. The worker who had been handling the child talked with us telling all she knew about him and his background, asking more questions, concluding with, "Would you like to see him?"

Eagerly, we answered, "Yes!"

We returned to our motel where he would visit us. How nervous we were! We had been told to bring an outfit, diapers, and six empty bottles. So, we got those out and had them available. We took the diaper bag and unpacked it then repacked it. What would we do? More important, what would he do? No woman in labor has even been through a more anxious time, no prospective father in a waiting room has ever paced more! Finally, we heard a car and there in the worker's arms was the most beautiful baby boy we had ever seen. His hair, what there was of it, was blond like mine. His eyes were blue, like mine. He was beautiful! Most important, he looked at me and then at Charles and smiled the most beautiful bright smile either of us had ever seen. I spoke, held out my arms and he came to me, and just as eagerly to Charles. In that moment, our cup ran over!

She left him with us after examining the things we had brought for him, telling us that she would return to pick him up. She went on to say that we should spend the night discussing the situation and deciding if we wanted to take this baby home with us. Then, she left.

We were alone with him for three hours. We took off all of his clothes—why? I do not know. I think we just wanted to know that he was real. We fed him, changed him, played with him, and while he slept, we sat and watched him. We called him Mike. The name we had selected for our baby, John Michael, means "beloved gift of God." He liked it. More important, he liked us. Then, she returned to take him away. Knowing that we would see him again, that God was preparing this for us, we still experienced a sense of loss. We could only pray for the time to go by quickly. We were instructed to discuss it and if we reached the decision to take him, we should be at the office at nine the next morning. We did not need the night to think, but we did think, and we prayed and we waited. At nine the next morning we were at the office where she asked, "Do you want him?"

As one, we answered, "Yes!" With that, we left to get ready for our baby, to pack and to wait, to become a family!

Finally, into that motel room came that bright smile, that beautiful little boy, now almost ours. We changed his clothes for those we had brought with us. Words do not tell how he looked in those clothes we had so carefully chosen. Charles picked him up and asked, "Ready to go home, Mike?" He snuggled into Charles's arms and we knew that our decision had been right. I gave the worker the clothing we had removed and six empty baby bottles. She gave me six bottles filled with formula in exchange. Having come here empty, we were leaving full, unable to comprehend that after so many years of waiting, we had our baby! Our God is so good.

At home, we introduced Mike to his room without seeing the first tear. Seemingly, he was happy with the whole arrangement. People began to come to the house. Calls became more numerous as word spread. Mike doted on the attention and the people. We telephoned his grandparents 250 miles away to tell them the news. We got him to sleep with no trouble, no tears, and then on our knees beside his bed, we thanked God for this great miracle, in many ways greater than the miracle of birth. We also dedicated the life of this child to God, who had made it all possible. That night, we heard his every move, but all of our anxiety was senseless. Mike seemed to know he was home.

Sunday, he went to church. He slept through most of the first sermon that he heard his daddy preach, not realizing that his daddy was preaching that Sunday with inspiration from a little boy, choosing as his text, "Let us receive the adoption of sons," (Genesis 4:5 KJV) a perfect parallel for salvation.

Mike grew up so quickly, accepting his role as the "preacher's son." He went to God's House, sitting quietly (occasionally) on the back pew. He always said his blessing which was "Thank you God for my supper," three times a day. He never met a stranger. At night as he was put to bed, he concluded his "now I lay me down to sleep. . ." prayer with, "God bless Mommy and Daddy." This prayer is still being answered daily. We are so blessed. Hallelujah!

Still, we clung to the hope that someday we would conceive a child. When Mike was two years old, I had surgery for the endometriosis and that hope was erased forever. During these long days of recuperation, I frankly faced the fact that I would never carry Charles's child within my body. We discussed it only once, agreeing that the only things that made that knowledge possible to bear was Mike and the knowledge of God's love. There awaiting our care and guidance was our child. We knew that we had done everything possible to have a child, but could not. God have given him to us. Now, all hope was gone. My doctor allowed Mike to visit me and my questions were answered, this was our child!

When we made it known that we had applied for placement of a child, we met some criticism. Some felt that we were wrong to bring "someone else's child" into the family. Some in our church field frankly disapproved. Oddly enough, these critics became Mike's honorary aunts and uncles. We never sought to overcome those objections. Mike did that with his charming personality, ability to adjust and that precious smile. He melted the hearts of the strongest objectors with a "how you doin' this morn'?" and shaking hands "like daddy." Jesus himself said, "A little child shall lead them." This one came into our lives leading.

The authorities urged us to tell Mike that he was adopted. This child who so proudly pointed to the pulpit and said, "That's my daddy preaching about God," who embraced us both so often saying, "I wuv you Mommy" or "I wuv you Daddy," must be told that we were not his Mommy and Daddy by conception, but by adoption. He had to know that somewhere he had another mother and father. His favorite bedtime story became the story of his adoption. How touching it was to hear this toddler say, "Tell me I'm 'dopted." One of us always obliged by telling him how badly we wanted a little boy and how God said, "I cannot let you have one, but I will help you find one." And how we chose him from all of the little boys and girls to be ours because we loved him. With sleepy eyes, he would look up and say, "Uh, huh, you wuv me," and drop off to sleep. He knew early that "adoption" is a word meaning warmth, love, happiness, safety, and security.

Biologically, we are not parents. We know however, the anxiety of sleepless nights when fever rages; the irritability of clothes that get too small overnight; the joy of Christmas morning when Santa gives that smile new radiance; the pride of first word, first step; all the joys of parenthood. True, they were not made possible by the accident of conception, but then according to William Cowper, "God moves in mysterious ways His wonders to perform".

Three years after Mike came to live with us, this beautiful experience was repeated in our lives. Having lived through the desolation of wanting a child so badly, then the euphoria of finding Mike, I never thought that any experience in this world—or any other—would be akin to it and evoke the same feelings from me. We had discussed it and agreed that we could support and love another child just the same as Mike. Discussing it, we decided that a brother would be perfect since they would be close in age. I had a sister two years younger than me and we had a wonderful relationship. So, we decided to apply again and to ask for another little boy. Having taken six months to find Mike, we figured that would be the same for our next child. So, we went through all of the home inspections, health reports, financial revelations—the entire process again. When we were approved, we told Mike that he was going to have a baby brother. He was enchanted. The three of us discussed the coming little boy. We talked about his toys and his bed and what he would like to eat. A name was important. After much discussion, we decided to name the new little boy, James Mark: meaning, "follower of my brother." So, we talked about Mark while Mike had begun talking about his "brudder" with real anticipation.

Six months passed and no word on a baby. Mike would ask about him daily. Then, I suppose that the newness or reality wore off and he rarely talked about the new baby. We had purchased an outfit in which to bring him home, and Mike had selected new baby toys for him. All of this was arranged in the room that would belong to the baby. But time was not working for us.

Finally, after a year, our social worker came to tell us that they had found a little boy. We were elated. This baby boy was nine months old and had been living in a foster home since birth. Oh my, there was no holding us back! The only question was how soon we could pick up this baby and make him ours.

Two weeks later, we made the trip again. This time, we had company. Mike was in the back seat talking constantly about going to get his little brother. He had a toy that he had selected for his brother and held it in his lap, even napping holding onto it. Finally, we were ready to see this new baby. Unlike with Mike, this social worker had the three of us come to an office where we were ushered into a darkened room and directed to look through a one way mirror at the little boy playing on the floor with another social worker. We were entranced. We held Mike up to the window and asked him, "Who is that?" With no hesitation, still clutching the toy, he said, "That's my baby brudder, Mark!" He was smiling and reaching for him. This made the social worker happy, so we were taken into the room where Mark was playing.

Instantly, Mike was on the floor handing the little boy the toy. Mark looked up at Mike with big, solemn dark brown eyes, and slowly took the toy. No smile, just an acceptance. The two of them played. Mark was a little taken aback as if he did not quite understand this boy coming into his playtime. Slowly, though, he did interact and smiled the sweetest most gentle smile that I had ever seen in my life. I picked him up and sat down to talk to him. When I looked into those eyes, I just melted. Tears just flowed down my face. I had found my child. Charles took him and Mark drew back and looked at him so seriously as if he were asking, "Who in the world are you?" He looked back at me once. Mike came to Charles's knee and said, "It's alright, he's our Daddy!" Talk about the nearness of God, He was there in that room building us a family.

Leaving Mark that evening to go back to the hotel and "think" about it was more difficult than one could ever imagine. Mike was heartbroken and kept asking where his "brudder" was and why we had left him. He was very disappointed in us. We had never left him and he could not understand why we were leaving Mark. Finally, we convinced him that Mark had to go back and pack up his things so that he could come and live with us. That seemed to calm him down. That night as we put him to bed he said, "Promise me that we are going to get my brudder in the morning." We promised. If only he knew how important that was to us, he would have been amazed.

Convincing Mike that we could not go for the baby until he had some breakfast, he finally stopped long enough to eat. Then off we went. The social worker had Mark and his things ready for us. He was wearing a pair of red corduroy overalls and a red and white striped shirt with little white leather shoes. We were given those clothes and a bag with some small toys and four bottles of formula. We did not have to leave empty bottles this time. When the time came for Charles and me to sign the papers, Mike insisted that he wanted to sign too for his brudder. So, the worker gave him a pen and he scribbled what he said was his name. Mark now belonged to him, he thought. With that, we were ready to go home. We had our second son—James Mark. With the two boys, we set off for the five hour ride home. They played, slept, and spent time just looking at one another.

While Mike looked so much like me, Mark had all of the attributes of his father's family. His eyes were dark, warm, mellow, serious brown, exactly like his father. He had some thin light brown hair that almost exactly matched Charles. (We never dreamed that his hair would wind up being as black as black could be and a thick as any I have ever seen.) Temperamentally, Mark is more like me—serious, quiet, and intense. He was nine months old and just exactly the right size for a child that age. When he cried, it was not loud and ear splitting like Mike: Mark's little face would wrinkle up and his mouth make a tight, little "O" and the tears would flow. This broke my heart. He had no idea who we were, and here he was cooped up in the car with the two of us and another little boy. I sat in the back seat with him, holding him or letting him play on the seat beside me. Mike would climb back and forth to play too. Mark would look at me so solemnly with those big brown eyes, and my heart would leap. When he slept, he was in my lap with his bottle firmly holding my finger. I felt like an anchor for him. He looked so sweet asleep. His brown hair was a bit tousled, his long, long eye lashes brushing his fair skin, and he looked so very innocent. Watching him sleep, I promised God that I would do everything in my power to make this little boy happy that he belonged to us. That is a vow that I maintain even today.

Once at home, we introduced Mark to his new room: the room that had been Mike's who now had his own "big boy bed" in another room. There were toys, diapers, clothes, everything that a little boy would need. I carried Mark into the room and he looked around with those big, dark eyes and took everything into his mind. Mike was showing him this and that and keeping a running dialog going. I do believe that by this time Mark had become accustomed to Mike and his running commentary. At any rate, Mike gave

Mark his first bottle in his new home. And, the whole story repeated itself.

Mark was such a good baby. Even that first night, he never cried at being put to bed and lights turned off. He loved to sleep. His naps would run long, so long that Mike would become anxious that something was wrong with him. He was very quiet. He played with toys and played with Mike. He responded to both Charles and me just like a happy, little boy, but he really responded to Mike. There was immediate and loving acceptance.

In church, Mark was as quiet as could be. Shortly after he came to us, we began a Nursery ministry so that babies could be left there during the morning worship service. Mark stayed there through Sunday school and church each Sunday. I would visit between the services to be sure that all was well. I still could not believe that he belonged to us. Such a perfect little boy was nothing short of a miracle.

Years proved that home and sibling relationships are truly gifts from God. Even tied down with diapers and babies, it was not impossible to see God's love. Two little boys who would more than likely never have met became brothers in the highest sense of the word. They would fight with each other but they make up and love each other. If anything, we grew closer to God, our salvation became more real and the brotherhood of man more important because of the relationship we saw develop between those two boys.

Mark was about two years old when God called Charles to another church about 150 miles away. Moving was a real experience with those two little ones. Charles was busy tying up loose ends at the church and with the association, so packing was my job. As soon as I would get a box packed, the two of them would unpack it. Mike was the ringleader but Mark was a great follower. When I would get Mark down for a nap—Mike had given up naps when he was a baby—I would encourage Mike to HELP me. That worked to some extent, but it was only after they were both in bed at night that I really got things done.

So, we moved again. Where the boys had had separate rooms now they would have to share a room. We had purchased twin beds when we took Mike out of the baby bed, so we were prepared. They were hilarious on that first night. Both of them wondered at the different house and all of the boxes and strange activities. As the church people came to greet us, bringing food and offers to help, the boys were both on their best behavior. Mark is such a smart person and was a very smart little boy at the time. He would greet each newcomer by holding out his hand to shake. He did not say a word but that was his greeting. The people were in love with him from the beginning. Mike was more interested in getting the swing set assembled and put up in the back yard. I think that was his lifeline. He enlisted a couple of men who came with offers to help and got them working on it. When it was done, he came in to tell Mark, "Now, we can play!" Off they went to something that was familiar to them.

This new church field proved to be one of the most interesting and friendly we ever encountered. From the first day onward they accepted us as their church family and the boys as our children. Life was good.

When Mike was in first grade and Mark was three, Charles became insistent that we explore adopting a little girl. I was thirty three years old, just finally rid of diapers and bottles and really not all that enthusiastic. He was definite. He wanted a little girl. I had three younger sisters; so, I already knew about little girls. Praying long and hard about it, I figured it out and decided in my heart that it would take so long to go through the process that we would both be beyond the accepted age to be awarded a child by the time one was found. The law specified that the mother be under 35. I was 34. So, I agreed. We applied for a little girl and set the wheels in motion. All of the inspections, reports, information, health tests and now with two little boys to add to the mixture were completed yet again. Imagine my chagrin when three months later we had a visit from our social worker with the message that a little girl had been found for us!

She explained to us that they had found a three month old little girl for us. She had no hair at all, but her parents were both blonde. She had blue eyes and fair skin. From birth, she had been in only one foster home. She was totally healthy and quite alert. We were to visit her within the week.

We had not even begun to get the boys prepared for a sister, nor made specific purchases for a little girl. Everything went into high gear. While I had not been enthusiastic over this at the beginning, I became a dynamo! I began to make lists—what to buy, what to do to the house to get ready, what to do about our commitments, and how to tell the boys. That was the easiest one. That night at supper, we told them that we were going to get another baby. Mike was all for it having been through it already with Mark. Mark was a little puzzled, but if Mike was for it, so was Mark—that had become his pattern, always follow Mike. Mike explained about what getting a new brudder entailed. We had to explain that this would not be a brudder but a sister. They both looked at us so seriously; "sister" was a new word for them. So, we had to explain that the relationship was the same, just she was a girl. Not too excited about a girl, they sensed that this was going to be special. Then, we set about preparing a room for the new baby.

We had only three bedrooms in this house. One was ours, one belonged to the boys, and the other was a guest room complete with a bedroom suite and all that was required to make it comfortable. With nowhere to put that bed, we set up the baby bed alongside the other bed. Since the room was large enough, this became satisfactory not only to me but to the boys. The little chest to hold clothing and other items just fit under the window and we could place the baby mural and other things on the wall above the side of the bed. It worked! To include the boys, I let them help me put the baby bed together. Working together, they lifted the mattress onto the bed and promptly, both of the climbed into the baby bed. After all, each of them had already occupied it themselves. I was having no luck explaining that this was not going to be another brudder, but a sister. Neither of them understood.

The next day, I took them with me to a neighboring town to shop for the baby. I must admit that buying clothes for a little girl was such a sweet experience. On a budget, I labored over my decisions. The boys of course had their input, especially when it came to toys. Finally, with what I thought was a decent beginning we went home. As I unpacked our purchases and explained the dresses to them, both of them were wide eyed. They looked at each other like I was telling them some weird story. Neither of them could understand why there were no pants! We had come up with a name overnight: Beverly Charlaine. "Beverly" is my first name, and "Charlaine" was an adaptation of Charles. Telling the boys this, neither of them could really understand such a name. I wrote it down and showed it to them. Mike promptly said, "I feel sorry for her. She will never be able to spell that!" (He had mastered "Mike" easily, "Burgess" not so much.) They just used "Baby" to refer to her.

Within a few days we were off to pick up our baby with both boys in the back seat. Mike, having been through all of this before, was excited and telling Mark what to expect. With this unexpected information and hastening to get everything ready, none of us could really anticipate what happened. When we arrived at the offices, the social worker chatted with the four of us briefly before taking us into an attractive play room where there was a worker with a tiny baby feeding her a bottle. Both boys went eagerly to see the baby even though we had cautioned them about overwhelming her. No need, as it turned out. With big blue eyes wide open she looked at both boys and continued taking her bottle as if there was really no big deal here. As Charles and I approached, I could see that this was the most beautiful little girl that I had ever seen.

She had absolutely no hair: yes, she was totally bald. Big blue eyes were taking in everything that was going on. She had the fairest complexion, and was dressed in a little pink dress with embroidered roses and smocking at the top. She was wearing little white booties with white socks. I not only thanked God for bringing us here, I thanked him for making her so beautiful and happy. When the bottle was finished, I took her in my arms and she looked at me with her eyes so wide. I sat her on my lap and patted her on the back and she gave a great big burp then smiled a tiny little smile, but, oh so sweet. The boys were in awe! They were not allowed to burp. Right then, they knew that she was special; while they were not allowed to burp, she could get praised for it. "Yes, she was special," they thought.

We took her home with us. Yes, we had to stay one night and convince the boys that she was going to be ours; but, when we had jumped through all of the hoops, I took her again and we went home. They gave us only the clothes she was wearing: a little white dress and booties with socks and four bottles of formula. By now, we were accustomed to all of this, and feeling like experienced veterans, we started the long drive back home. I was sitting in the back with the baby and Mark. Mike was on his knees in the passenger seat in front. We had been on the road for about an hour when he proclaimed, "We have to take her back! Turn around, Daddy; we have to take her back." Horrified, I asked him why. He told me that we had to take her back because she was not a girl. "We wanted a girl!" he said. Finally, we got him to tell us that the trouble was the people had promised him a sister but this was not a girl because she had no hair! He was right—no hair. But, we did get him to accept that she would have hair eventually.

Until this very day, both boys have teased her about having no hair. Even when she was a teenager with too much hair; that was still their joke. Mark constantly tells her that Mike wanted to take her back! She still laughs about it.

When we got Charlaine home and into the nursery we had prepared for her, the boys hung onto the side of her baby bed never wanting to leave her. They took turns giving her the bottle and had to be shooed out of the room for her diaper changes. Again, the members of our church came with food and gifts for the new baby and good wishes for all of us. The boys took pride in showing her off and telling them that she had no hair but really was a girl! Charlaine, like Mark, was never any trouble. She took her new environs in stride and responded to all four of us just like she had always known us. She was a dream in church. Even though we had a nursery, I insisted on keeping her with me. Having been so reluctant to go through the adoption of a little girl, I was totally in love with this baby.

My parents who lived about 100 miles away drove down the next week to see their new granddaughter. She won them over in nothing flat. She smiled and held on to my father and allowed my mother to feed and bathe her. Almost like she knew that these were special people for her life, she was drawn to them. They brought her a box full of clothes. My mother felt so sorry when she heard about my hurry up shopping, that she outdid herself. One of the best pictures that I own is my father on the floor with Charlaine with both of them smiling and so happy. A special affinity was established that day that lasted until his death five years later. His last time with Charlaine was four days before he died when he sat with her on his lap and read to her. She still remembers that day and her "Papa."

About two weeks later, the ladies of the church gave her a shower at the home of one of our ladies who lived nearby. I dressed her in one of the outfits my mother had brought: a little pink top with rose appliques and a lace collar with pink diaper cover to match along with little pink shoes that matched exactly and white socks. She looked adorable. At the shower, she was passed from lady to lady all around the room. Presents! There were so many and there were even more clothes as well as practical things like diapers and furniture, everything that a new mother needs for a little girl. In the middle of opening the gifts, she dropped off; sound asleep in the arms of my friend. We took her into the adjoining bedroom and placed her in the middle of the bed with pillows on both sides of her. She took a deep breath and did not care one bit that she was the center of attention. That is how she has lived her life until this very day. Her father cherished her, her brothers adore her, but, I love her!

Our children are a gift from God, evidence of His concern for us and His confidence in us. More importantly, they are daily proof to us that God answers prayer. Hallelujah!

Our children have always been very special to both of us. To me, there is a meaning words will not describe. There have been times when I wanted to tear out my hair in desperation because of these three. There have also been times when my spirit soars in gratitude for these same three. So many times, preacher's kids walk a difficult road. Perfection is expected by the church congregation and the school. They stay on the proverbial "hot seat." They must be perfect to be accepted by adults and that same perfection earns them hard times from their peers. I have seen all three of my children suffer, literally, when they were the only ones in their age group at a church service. Praise God. I have seen the same three square their shoulders and start the enlistment campaign that evolves a successful organization. I have hurt for my children, rejoiced for them, and felt total bewilderment as well. Variously, I have written a tribute, of sorts, for each child. To emphasize their part in Ruth's life, I include one such article for each of my children.

FOR OUR OLDEST SON—MICHAEL

As a girl, I learned that the eagle was special—a symbol of America, exuding pride and confidence while implying strength. Never, not in my wildest dreams, did I visualize myself the mother of an eagle—but, I am and very proud of it.

In July of 1969, Michael was eight years old. The world was caught up in man walking on the moon. Michael sat enraptured before the television set as this real life adventure unfolded. On the night when Neil Armstrong stepped out of the "Eagle" onto the surface of the moon, we had awakened Michael and brought him in to sit sleepily and witness this miracle of history. This was important! Not just because of history, but because of Michael.

Upon the advent of his awareness of toys, he always loved planes, space vehicles, rockets, and anything that gave man wings. Thus, the moon landing was important to him. As he watched the drama unfold, Neil Armstrong became his hero. Michael was impressed with the fact that Mr. Armstrong was an Eagle Scout, and with the number of astronauts who had scouting backgrounds, he set his sights on becoming an Eagle Scout en route to becoming an astronaut.

I suppose that in his young mind, he equated it with the flying he so dearly loved. But, as the years unrolled, the work, the devotion, and the goal remained. He never deterred. Years later, when we considered accepting a church in another town, Mike's first question involved scouting. Fortunately, the town to which God was leading had an active scout troop into which Mike could transfer. (I have often wondered what would have been his feelings had there been no active program. Thank goodness, we did not have to face that.)

Soon after the Eagle landed on the moon, Mike joined a Cub Scout group forming in our town and advanced quickly through the work, quickly becoming a Bobcat, Wolf, Bear and nine Webelo badges. God then led us to a church in a town without scouting. Mike did not check this out before the move as he would later do. He determined that there would be a program there in which he could continue toward his goal. By this time, his goal had caught our imagination as well.

Busy getting into the work of a new church, a new school, and a new community, we gave the matter low priority. To our door one day came the District Scout Executive recruiting adult leadership to begin scouting in our town. Quickly, I sensed a power higher than I at work and volunteered to work with the Cub Scouts. I learned that no one had been secured to work with the Boy Scouts. Mike went to work and at our organizational meeting there were eleven boys recruited by Mike along with a Scoutmaster. Many scoffed that this would never work, but signed up their sons anyway. They did not buy uniforms because they did not believe. Michael did.

He immediately purchased his Scout Handbook and went to work. Within three months he had earned the awards for Tenderfoot plus! Serving as Den Chief for the Cub Scouts, he trained the boys on advancement and helped with the handwork, planned and conducted the games and loved it all. He incorporated all of his hobbies—the outdoors, aviation, bugs, snakes, nature, and art into merit badges and became the most decorated scout in his troop.

He helped others too. Each Saturday there would be a group at our house and Mike would be helping them to earn their badges. A Court of Honor was held when a sufficient number of boys had earned their awards. Mike received his Tenderfoot rank on his father's birthday. His dad was away in a revival and unable to attend, but wrote Mike a letter of congratulations that was placed in his scrapbook. This was the first step toward Eagle.

At Boy Scout camp, he earned the canoeing merit badge, much to our surprise, for he had never seen a canoe! He began Archery, but being left handed, he had some trouble. Later, at Royal Ambassador Camp in a wilderness situation, he finished up.

By this time, he was among the highest ranked Royal Ambassadors in the state and working on his National Achievement. His father had been skeptical about scouting, fearing that it would interfere with Royal Ambassadors, but it added a new dimension. I believe that it was this dual force that led Mike to his God and Country Award so early.

Mike began this work as soon as he was eligible while keeping up his R. A. work, his scouting merit badge work, activities as Den Chief, playing football, and even doing better in school. By nature, Mike is shy and not outspoken. When he appeared before the deacons, his dad confided that he was amazed at his reactions to their questions and eagerness to talk. Mike was the first scout from his troop to earn his God and Country Award, and the first in the history of his church. He was so happy. His troop was there in uniform. The Cubs were there in uniform, the Troop, Pack, and American flags were there with all of his friends. He was scared when told that he would have to make a speech. So, being a good mother, I helped him write one. Imagine my surprise, when it came his turn and he spoke from his heart and it was so much better than what we had written.

His picture appeared on the front page of the county paper and he got letters from people in the church, our congressman, the senator, but the one he prizes most is from the president of the Southern Baptist Convention.

At this time, we made the move into which he inquired about scouting. By now, he was involved in choosing and Eagle project. His first idea was to set up a Royal Ambassador program in our new church, where there had never been one. That was accomplished and the men of the church were led by the Lord to take it over. Mike confided that he did not feel right counting that, and had decided to clean up the church cemetery. We discouraged this until we heard his reason. My sister had died two years earlier, and he wanted this cemetery as nice as "Aunt Bobbye's." That did it. We backed off and gave help as he asked.

He not only cleaned it up but took pride in keeping it that way. He checked on all funerals and personally supervised the situation whenever possible. This became his responsibility rather than a project. The Scout Oath and Law had become a part of him.

The night that he was examined by the committee for his Eagle rank, his father and I were nervous. Michael coolly carried all of his work and sat there hearing that he had passed well. Awaiting national acceptance was routine. When informed that he was accepted and the date had been set for his Court of Honor that smile gleamed so widely!

On that night, he seemed to grow by inches. Going to the front to receive his award with us at his side, there was a new awareness. Out little boy of 1969 was a young man now. A dream come true. There was no doubt. He even let me hug him—and that was usually a no no. Later, at home, I walked by the door to his room and found him quietly sitting there looking at his medal. My eyes clouded with tears as I thought of all those years of work and wondered if he was counting the cost. Seeing me, he said, "Mother, I am an Eagle Scout. I will never do anything to have this taken from me. Do you know how important it is?" And he honored that commitment. He earned more badges: he went to camp, earned two palms and had enough awards for two more. He still worked and encouraged his brother. His little sister wanted to be an Eagle Scout too. We had a hard time explaining to her why she had to go by way of Brownies.

So, I am the mother of an Eagle. That is such a good feeling. I am so thankful to God what that meant to my son.

Michael encountered many problems in his life. Some of them he handled well, and some not quite so well. He graduated from high school and went to college on a scholarship to study Art.

When he was twenty one, he went to work as a Correctional Officer with the Georgia Department of Prisons. At this time, God led us to move to another church in another part of the state. Michael moved into an apartment with a friend. Not quite a year later, we got word that Mike had been assaulted by one of the prisoners there for a life term and was hospitalized. His physical wounds were taken care of, but his mental wounds never healed. He went back to work at the prison but had so many flashbacks that he was moved to another facility. That worked for a few years until there was an uprising that caused his mental block to return. He was put on Workman's Compensation and came to live with us until things were better for him.

He was there for over a year seeing a psychiatrist weekly and working on getting his mental health back. During this time, my husband—his father—passed away which was another blow to Michael. Mark was working away at that time, so only Charlaine and I were left at home when Michael determined to go back to work. The Department assigned him to a facility in South Georgia and then to one near my home. But, all of the problems caught up with him and he was retired from the Prison System. With his own apartment, his bills paid, and friends and family nearby, we thought that Michael would finally be able to put all of that behind him. But, in June of 2010, Michael passed away. His last years had been so mentally and emotionally challenging that all of us concluded that God had been merciful and that now Michael could be at peace, finally.

My heart soared as my other son, Mark, gave Mike's eulogy. The idea that these two would likely never have met had they not been adopted, yet were close brothers to the point that Mark wanted to do this amazed me even as it also broke my heart. But that is the kind of person Mark has become.

There are no words to tell you my feelings at that time. When Mike died, he took a part of my heart that had belonged only to him. While I still have the parts belonging to Mark and Charlaine, I have lost a part of me that cannot be replaced. He was my first baby. I shall never forget his first night in our home, his first bath, when he learned to walk, to read, and to walk into adulthood. I would not call him back if I could. God in His infinite mercy has made him whole again. Praise God! I am still the mother of an Eagle and thankful for his life. I am proud to be the mother of Michael and my broken heart still beats.

As a toddler, Mike had to have hernia surgery. His father having been called away for a funeral, I was alone when he went into the operating room. I sat praying alone when an older woman friend with whom I had worked in Associational WMU came by and recognized me. Explaining why I was there, my anxiety certainly showed. Helpfully, she touched my hand and said, "Well, darling, it's not like he is your real son." In that moment, I realized something that held true for all three children for all of these years. If I could have loved him anymore, I am glad that I did not give birth to him: I do not have that much more love. He was MY son in a cold operating room and God and I cared. I still care. My love for him has not decreased: my memories are so real and so special.

FOR OUR YOUNGER SON—MARK

"And Jesus increased in wisdom and in stature and in favor with God and man" Luke 2:52 KJV.

Where is my beautiful baby boy with the serious, mellow, dark, brown eyes? He was so late in learning to walk. Where is he now?

I sit here in this gym of a middle school watching a handsome lad charge up and down the basketball court. His jersey says "Burgess" and bears the number 12. My program says that this is our Mark. Can this be the little guy whom I rocked to sleep such a short time ago? We thought he was slow to pull up, stand alone, and walk. Now this boy fairly flies with the precious ball hitting the court beside him. As he leaps to sink the ball through the basket I cannot help but be amazed at the transformation.

Now, I sit on a cold aluminum seat in a football stadium of a high school watching number 45 who has the name "Burgess" on his back. My Mark! How he is growing up. The quarterback heaves the ball into space and twenty high school boys head down the field: ten are ours, ten are theirs. I look with fear and sure enough the ball is headed for my Mark. Without conscious thought, I ball my hands into fists, my nails digging into the flesh of my palms and I hold my breath. For an eternity the ball hangs above the boys and then drops—my Mark catches it over his shoulder and with a speed that I never anticipated, he heads for the end zone with a number of their guys after him. I am not breathing! If they tackle him, it will have to hurt! But, he runs—seemingly like the wind—and crosses the goal line. Without even realizing it, a yell escapes my lips and my arms rise in a sign of victory as I watch my son turn toward the stands with unadulterated joy on his face! This is our son. As his team converges on him to pound his back and shout in glee, I realize that tears are coming down my cheeks. What happened to my little boy? He is amazing!

At the outset of Mark's life with us, it was clear that he was unique. Never a crier or a whiner, he was a quiet child who showed affection and attracted attention because of his big, brown eyes and gentle way. Positive of what he wanted, he never settled for less, thus earning the title of "stubborn." Those in the know say that a middle child has a difficult life and many times lacks identity. Mark may have had some tough times. I know this, his father knows this and Mark knows this. With a creative brother and sister,

Mark's talent was not of this bent, yet he enjoyed their activities while doing his own thing. He took pride in their accomplishments yet maintained his own direction. Cheerfully wearing hand me down clothes from his brother, he gloried in the fact that he wore them a grade earlier than Michael and would therefore be taller and bigger when they are both grown.

Mark is smart. He sets goals for himself and undertakes them without any elaborate attention at all. He is quiet; but, he is rarely left out. His demeanor is smooth and consistent. The seriousness seen in his eyes and in his expression is very real. He is not creative but he is intelligent and smart as can be. What he undertakes is often amazingly advanced for him; but, he goes about it with such a serious intent that he has many, many admirers. His common sense is amazing as well.

As a fourth grader, he played football to please his dad, not because he wanted to play. Yet, he became the quarterback, the leader of his team and almost scored a touchdown. Challenged, he would wrestle and box, but preferred quieter activities and NEVER initiated physical encounters. An excellent student, he exercised his capacity to learn and became outstanding consistently making the Honor Roll.

While a fifth grader, he was selected to shadow the Principal for a day at his school for Career Day. Seeing his picture on the front page of the paper sitting behind that big desk looking so very "in charge," I knew that this one was going to do well and find his place in life. He has not disappointed me at all.

Success is a goal he eyes regularly. In elementary school he was always elected to some superlative honor as "friendliest," "most cooperative," or something to that effect. Teachers constantly nominated him for honors and selected him for recognition. In a large middle school, he was elected vice president of the Student Council, served on the annual staff, was in the Beta Club and held other offices. In the midst of that school year, his father was led to change churches. At first, Mark was reluctant, but as the time to move approached, he accepted the change. Sure enough, he picked up right where he left off—a favorite. That he could come into a new school, completely unknown and immediately receive recognition defies reality. Yet this actually happened. More importantly, he expected it to happen. This was something that he took for granted. Mark has always been just himself with no conceptions of grandeur or exaggerated self-esteem.

While he yearned to be nine years old in order to go to Royal Ambassador Congress, on his ninth birthday he underwent an emergency appendectomy, recuperating under the watchful eye of all of us, just in time to make the trip to camp. Mark was the epitome of what every church dreams of in a Royal Ambassador. He loved the organization. Camp was special to him. We knew there was a unique feeling about R.A. camp and appreciated that fact. The real specialness was manifested when it was at camp that he surrendered his life to the will of God. In discussing his decision with us, he seriously confided his intention to "be a pro basketball player until my legs give way, and then I'll be a preacher." Talk about having priorities in order!

He excelled in working through that organization and during his senior year of high school, he was recognized by the Southern Baptist Convention for his achievements and elected to serve as a Page at the Convention in their annual meeting in New Orleans. The Royal Ambassador magazine featured an article about him and his accomplishments not only in RAs, but in school, and in his life. There was a full page picture of him as well. He really is a role model for younger boys.

As a seventh grader, he had set his goal to play basketball for his school. Admitting the abundance of "bigger boys" who had experience, he attended the first practice session—along with sixty other boys. Upon hearing the conditions for play and the schedule for practicing, he adjusted his study and church activities accordingly. Keeping his grades higher than ever before, he valiantly attended EVERY practice and forced his body into arduous exercises. The odds were against him: no experience, not the biggest and strongest, unknown, new. Determination is his long suit. Many of the others dropped out. Mark stayed. The day came for the cut and he prepared himself to be a casualty. Not so! Bursting into the kitchen he glowed his news—"I made it!" Quickly he followed up with, "I know that I won't play much, but I'll learn a lot." In reality, his most valuable lesson was already learned.

I was so proud of him! I felt his joy; and, I felt his accomplishment. My mind and my heart returned to that long ago playroom and that serious eyed little boy who was so quiet and unassuming. Leaping ahead, I remembered how he had lived his years with quiet determination and an eagerness to accomplish his goals. I was so joyous for him at attaining this goal no matter how elusive it might have been. Confident, on that day, I knew that Mark would make his mark in life and that it would be a good one.

Joy is the only word describing this day in our son's life. Wearing the hallowed blue and white uniform and brand new twenty dollar shoes, he bounded out of the locker room onto the basketball court. Unbelievably his older brother had used his own allowance to pay the admission charge to see Mark's first game. I wondered if it was pride or curiosity. Carefully, he avoided looking at us. Soon we knew why—he was a starter! A skinny seventh grader with big brown eyes and a healthy crop of black hair, wearing our son's name lined up with the big boys and began the realization of his dreams.

Mark went on to play middle school basketball and shine. In high school, he played both varsity basketball and football even toying with tennis for a bit. He was outstanding in both of his sports and academically as well. In his senior year he was accorded many honors and served on the Model UN. A full page picture of him in the yearbook declares him "Mr. Metter." He still keeps up with his high school friends. Mark's move to a new school had not deterred him at all. In fact, the move might just have been the best thing for him.

When he became too old for R. A. camp, he became a counselor. Every one of his summers through college was given to camp. He oversaw the water activities, was a certified life guard, counseled the boys, and helped in every way. The most significant of his contributions was the life that he modeled for them. He still counts those among the best times of his life. That is where he really grew up.

Serious about his family, he was always easily the favorite of both grandmothers. He knows that he can get his heart's desire with those big eyes. One of his grandmothers regularly prepared scrambled eggs and cinnamon toast for him when he is there while she gave the other children cold cereal. (He was constantly teased about this, but he did not care.) The other grandmother prepares macaroni and cheese and bought him special gifts. His childless aunt, my sister Bobbye, took him for an afternoon outing with her husband on their boat and they were special to him for the rest of her life. Not given to affection for children, she sent a packet of snapshots airily inscribed, ". . . and a good time was had by ALL." Her early death while Mark was still very young was a real blow to him. He had lost someone who had really touched his life. This was his first encounter with the death of a loved one. Just a year later when told of the untimely death of my father, his beloved "Papa, tears welled in those precious eyes, but he turned away, "too big to cry."

Mark graduated from high school and went on to college where he had a tough time with studying and being away from home while maintaining his friendships with the boys and girls alike. He pledged a fraternity and played basketball with them. He served as a lifeguard and totally enjoyed the experience. Graduating from college, he spent a year trying to decide what he really wanted to do before he settled into a job with a local college as a Resident Hall Manager.

While he was working there, we discovered that Charles had cancer. Mark became my strongest support. With absolutely no tears or emotion except in his eyes, he was there for me and for Michael and Charlaine. Perhaps, I leaned on him too heavily; but, he never complained. Each time the doctor would give me a report, Mark would telephone to know what it was. He wanted no detail spared. In a serious relationship with his college sweetheart, he was always there when I needed him seemingly.

As the years have passed, he has continued to be my very strong support. He is not emotional, but very determined. I have been reprimanded by him more than once for not following HIS rules! This just makes me smile.

When there was a bit of improvement in Charles and he wanted to go to the mountains "one more time," I drove him there giving the children the weekend on their own. At this time, we knew that Charles was terminal. Once we got to the house and settled in, he seemed so comfortable and relaxed that I knew we had done the right thing. He slept well that night and into the morning. We had a relaxed that day and watched the World Series. Just after dark, he hemorrhaged and had to be taken to the local hospital by ambulance. At the doctor's suggestion, I called the children. I could not find Mark. After many telephone calls and much prayer, I called the mother of his girlfriend who told me that Mark was out in the middle of the lake with Jill and her father night fishing. She promised that she would have him call me when they came back. He called about midnight. I told him what had happened and asked him to leave in the morning, to go by our house and pick up Michael and Charlaine and to be careful. I should have known better. Mark and Jill, his girlfriend, drove all of the way that night. At the hospital, Mark was very serious so that when the doctor presented us with choices, we were ready to take the steps that we needed to take. The doctor advised that Charles needed more care than was available at this small hospital and that he was terminal. We arranged for an ambulance to take him to the hospital where we lived. Mark was there for me. He drove my car home as we followed the ambulance on what would be Charles's last trip.

Mark visited his father daily, helping him to eat and even shaved him. No one could have been more attentive. I knew that on that Thursday, he had an interview for an excellent position with a national company; however, when I called him to tell him that the doctors suggested that we all get there and directed him to come straight from his interview, I was not at all surprised to see him walk into the hospital room shortly, having informed the interviewers that he would have to put it off. He was at his father's side with us when his father died. He drove me home that day. There were no tears and little conversation.

During that afternoon, his girlfriend drove into our drive and Mark went out to meet her. I stood in the den—I don't know what I was thinking. But, I saw her get out of the car and Mark met her as she took him into her arms. I could see his body shaking and I knew that he was weeping. Tears in my own eyes told me how deeply affected he had been, but how he had held it all together for the sake of his family. He had been there for me. He had been strong and caring. Now, he could let go. What an experience that was! I knew then how much he cared for her.

He drove my car to the church for the funeral, in the procession to the cemetery, and he was at my elbow when the sod was put onto the casket. He never left me. His strength was there for me and the others during the adjustments and affairs that needed to be handled. Somewhere in that time, he had his interview and he got the job. My son deserved it—and more.

Mark married that girl, Jill. She is a wonderful girl—emotional, fun loving, sincere, smart, and all that I would wish for him. They are good together. While she flies off the handle quickly, he holds his tongue and quiets her fears. She is from a good family having been baptized as a child just like Mark. They have built a beautiful home filled with love and friends and happiness. She has a highly responsible job that requires much from her. She is able to do this because she knows that Mark is there for her. A beautiful girl on the outside, she is equally lovely on the inside. She is good to her parents and really cares about her friends.

Seven years into their marriage, she gave birth to Mark's son, my only grandchild, Jackson. He looks exactly like Mark. As he has gotten older, he does have his mother's eyes and the shape of her face, but he is so much like Mark that at times I can see that little boy in him. Jackson loves sports, but his favorite is baseball. So Mark has learned all that he can about baseball. Both Jill and Mark support Jackson one hundred percent in all that he undertakes. Jackson knows that he has their love and they want only the best for him. He is a lucky young man to have two such devoted parents to help him grow up and take his place in the world.

Just after the horror of 9/11, I took a really bad fall at my mountain house. I had several broken bones and a crushed elbow. Mark got the call from the local hospital. Although the Air Force Base where he works was on lock down because of the World Trade Center attack, he managed to get away to come to me. At the suggestion of the doctors, in the middle of the night, he bundled me into his vehicle and took me back to Macon and a specialist for surgery. The doctor gave him two pills to give to me when we got to the house in Macon. Dutifully, Mark put me to bed, gave me the pills, and spent the rest of the night there taking me to the doctor and the hospital the next morning.

After my surgery, Jill or her parents would stay with me during the day and Mark would spend the night until my daughter, Charlaine could get a plane out of Texas. Mark has come to the mountains to take me for cataract surgery and cranial surgery always staying until he feels that I can be up and about. He is the source of monumental strength for me.

My baby boy? He is there, hiding deep within jerseys for basketball and football teams, getting his degree and handling his life. Some days I see in my mind that little boy, so serious and determined, in that bed just barely making a dent in the covers; then, I see him now, a grown man who has lived his life, dreamed his dreams, and passing that determination onto his own son. Mark loves deeply and sincerely. Now, I see him as a father making the good decisions and working hard to make the world a better place. God has blessed him, for that I am so thankful.

I am grateful to God for Mark, for his life, his love, his family, his personality, and his success. I am also grateful to God for Mark's growth—in all ways. The tenderness I have for him in my heart knows no bounds. He is God's man and I love him.

Mark, you are loved for the little boy you were, for the awesome man you are, and the precious son you will always be.

FOR OUR DAUGHTER—CHARLAINE

The Bible tells us that Jehovah God has magnificent blessings in store for His children, those who claim His name and do His will. In the New Testament, Jesus promises us answers to our prayers as His Father, God's, unlimited blessings. Having read that all of my life and having given my heart to Him at age twelve and my life at age sixteen, I do not suppose that I ever really thought about what those "magnificent, unlimited blessings" would be like. However, God in all of His mercies takes care of us, and in spite of my ignorance, poured them out on us. In giving us our children, He did pour out those blessings and the essence of those blessings came in the form of our daughter, Charlaine.

When we brought her home, we declared her our princess. But, in her life, she has really and truly become a queen. We did her birth announcements like a royal invitation, declaring her our princess. Along the way, she has had some very unprincess moments, but also some very queenly times. All in all, watching that little baby grow up has been most revealing and rewarding.

From the beginning, Charles referred to her as his "darling." He would walk into a room and say "Where's Daddy's darling?" and she would run to him and jump into his arms. When she learned to talk, he would say to her, "Who is Daddy's darling?" She would say, "Me! I'm Daddy's darling!" And so life for her was associated with the first man in her life.

Mike and Mark saw to it that she learned to walk. Why bother with crawling? They were ready for a new playmate and she was it! So it was that though she was barely seven months old, they had her up and walking. She has never stopped since then.

The supreme mountaintop for any Ruth comes when all of those whom she loves are united in spirit and in truth. I have had this wonderful privilege several times. The two most significant occasions that lifted my spirit to new heights were the baptism of my children. Our boys were baptized together by their father. Their brotherhood seemed to be cemented when their dad brought them into the baptismal waters together, baptizing first Michael and then Mark. For the first time, he deviated from his litany saying, "I baptize you, my son. . ." Heaven seemed to come right down to us that night.

On the night that Charlaine was baptized, I had just lost my father. She was so small and very precious as she went into the baptismal waters to meet her beloved Daddy. She looked up at him and her little face shone with all of the love in the world. Deviating again, he said, "I baptize you my daughter. . ." As daddy's darling experienced the cleansing flood, I am sure that the angels in heaven enjoyed a mountaintop with me.

Charlaine continued to grow in wisdom, in grace, and in her love for others. Her childhood was spent trying to keep up with her brothers. To their credit, they included her whenever possible and some time when it should have been impossible. They taught her to ride her bicycle, to climb trees, to play with cars and trucks, and to play football. Yes, she was their buddy. When they wanted to play, she was always ready. Their friends accepted her as "one of the gang." She was even discovered one day wearing Mike's football shoulder pads!

But, she did like to play with the girls too. Not having a sister plagued her, so she was always inviting other girls to her house to play. She would even get on her bicycle and scour the neighborhood for a little girl with whom to play. Dolls were really not her thing. She only wanted to comb their hair. She became very angry with me when I stopped her from cutting their hair! She was not much into girly clothes either. On Sundays, I would dress her up with ruffles and bows and brand new white tights with her Mary James. She would return after church with her hair askew, sash untied, and her tights in tatters. Her explanation: "I was playing football!"

When she was only three years old, she captured her brothers' admiration when she sat down at the piano and played "Bad, Bad Leroy Brown." We were all stunned. She had a natural talent for music. Mark was taking piano lessons and struggling. He could not believe that she could just play like that.

A friend in a neighboring community took her as a piano student at that age and was amazed at her abilities. She loved music and was playing for church when she was only six years old. How she got to that spot is interesting. We had just moved to this church and she was getting accustomed to her new piano teacher who had become attuned to the fact that Charlaine had a unique talent, apparently. She had moved away from the music she normally gave to her six year old students and gave Charlaine some contemporary Christmas music to memorize and

play. That year, Charlaine was taken with the
song, "The Little Drummer Boy" and had picked
it out by ear on our piano. (Again impressing the
boys.) Ironically, the teacher gave her that
music. Before the next lesson, Charlaine had it
memorized which impressed the teacher who
suggested that she play it for church. Since we
were new to this church, we were reluctant to just
put her on the program. Charlaine, however, was
not so reticent. She went straight to the Minister
of Music and told him what her teacher had said.
The next Sunday she was on the program to play
her song. Because it was the Christmas season, I
had made her a little green dress with a
Christmas design. Of course, she chose to wear
that with her white patent "go go" boots. She did
look cute. When her turn came, she did a great
job. Her feet did not touch the pedals, but one of
the men in the congregation came to me and
observed that she kept time by swinging her feet.
I had never noticed. She played in that church
many times after that.

At the next church, she played frequently taking
turns with another pianist and did some solos as
well. Her voice was maturing and many of the
ladies loved to hear her sing. At the next church,
there was no pianist—the last preacher's
daughter had played for church, but she moved
with him. Quite naturally, Charlaine moved onto
the piano bench and had the task from then until
her father died at which time she was added to

the staff at another church in the town where she was amazed that they paid her! By this time, her voice was wonderful. She sang many solos and conducted the Children's Choir as well as playing for church and accompanying the choir.

Her high school chorus teacher loved working with her; so, she became the pianist for the school chorus and choir. During her eleventh grade year, the choir toured Europe giving concerts with Charlaine at the piano. On that trip she played in some of the great institutions of Europe. From ninth grade on, she was in the marching band playing the flute which she brought into her church music.

She has studied music for most of her life. In college, she majored in Piano Performance and minored in Voice. Her graduate degree is in Piano Performance. She has an amazing voice and has sung for many weddings and funerals. When she was studying opera, I was amazed at the strength of her voice. While studying the Gregorian chants, I was amazed at her ability to understand all of the various types of music. God gave her a wonderful talent and she has not been afraid to use it.

She did the work of a Minister of Music when she was old enough for the title. Receiving an inheritance from my mother at her death, she bought her own Grand Piano which graced our

Dining Room and where she taught Piano to her own students and practiced her music.

Throughout her teens, she remained consistent with her music and with her church. Many times, she found herself alone because she did not participate in certain activities. She maintained her Christian witness and in doing so met some very interesting people. She brought many dates to church, especially on Sunday night. Her date would sit in the pew she had shown him, and when she finished with the music, she would join him. This never seemed to bother them and made her a role model to many young women and men.

She put herself through four years of college accompanying the University Choir in their performances and on their tours, even the European one which saw her play in world famous cathedrals and halls. She loved her music and never found it to be a chore. At times the boys would get tired of hearing her practice, but they knew her talent too.

A very high compliment came her way when Mark and Jill asked her play and sing at their wedding. She also played for her cousin when she married in Baltimore. Known all over the area for her musical ability she was in great demand. God gave her so much talent and she was unafraid to use it.

When her father was hospitalized and dying, one night I was overcome with it all and sat down on my bed weeping at all that was being taken from him: that he would never see his children married, or meet any grandchildren. Charlaine came into the room and put her arms around me comforting me as no one else could have done reminding me that "God never gives us more than we can bear." She had become a woman of great faith. On that night, I realized that I would never be alone. This young woman would be there to support me and remind me about my faith and how good our God was to all of His children.

When Charles knew that he was dying, he planned his funeral. He did not ask for much, he was a humble man. The one thing that he really wanted was for Charlaine to play the piano for an interval of quiet time while she sang his favorite song. She could not sing: her heart, like the hearts of all of us, was broken. But she stood up and crossed the sanctuary to the piano with great dignity and played the song he had requested. There was total silence in the church. We all knew what a task this was and that she did it for her father. That is the young woman who still stands by me in dark times, in times of indecision, and when I need a "good talking to." Our relationship is one of which I could never have dreamed. We consult on all of my purchases, my clothes, my depression, and she kept Michael as straight as could be. When he died, she almost collapsed in Texas. She was on the first plane and was here with me for a few days after his Memorial Service. Even though she was hurting, she was concerned for me. I do not know what I would do without her. She has a wonderful husband, who does not hesitate to share her with me.

With a part time job while she was in college, she learned the profession of Archivist. We wondered where this would take her. When she completed her Bachelor's degree, she was hired full time at that job and promised raises and a good future at the Jimmy Carter Presidential Library. For four years after her father's death, she lived at home with me and commuted to school for her Master's and to her job.

Upon her graduation with her Master's degree, Charlaine moved to Texas—a thousand miles separated her from me. She was interviewed for and given the job of Archivist at the Lyndon B. Johnson Presidential Library. My heart was broken. I really thought that I could not survive without her. I had not realized how much I had come to depend upon her. I rode with her there when she moved so that she would not be alone on that move and to assure myself of her apartment and the people with whom she worked. I prayed so hard for this to be right—I could feel that God was leading her there. Needing to know that she was alright was heartening, but knowing that I was alright was something else. She had chosen a lovely apartment overlooking a canyon with room for her piano, and all of the comforts I would want for her. On the plane home, I cried all of the way, much to the consternation of all of the other passengers.

She saves her leave to come home a couple of times a year. I was going out there once a year until travel just got to be too much for me. She and Adam, her husband, enjoy coming to the mountains and just relaxing. He would move here today if they could.

Two years ago, I had a severe respiratory failure and was taken to the hospital on Christmas Day while they were here. Both of them did everything that they could for me. Adam even smuggled a Diet Coke and some Christmas cookies into the hospital. Scheduled to go back home three days later, Charlaine took three weeks of leave from her job and stayed with me. Adam returned home and kept in touch by phone. She did everything. Having become a really great cook, she made and froze meals so that I would not have to cook for a while after she did go home. All of my friends were so impressed with her and the good care she gave to me. She is not only my daughter but my best friend as well.

Her life has been successful. She went to school in Texas and earned a Master's in History to facilitate her promotions in her Archivist position. Traveling to conferences and training in various other libraries, she has learned so much. Her wisdom, intelligence, common sense, and amazing sense of self have served her well. She purchased her own three bedroom brick home years ago; traded cars, bought furniture, and sang with the Austin Symphony Chorus. She made a life for herself.

She met and married Adam Hester of Lubbock, Texas. Before they were engaged, I went to Texas to meet him. Thankfully, I approved. I am not sure what would have happened if I had not. Then, she brought him home to meet her brothers and sister in law as well as her nephew. He passed all of those tests too. We all prayed that this was a good move for her and that he would love her as she loved him. Then, we all prepared for the wedding at which Jackson was the ring bearer and Mark gave her away in his Father's place. Adam has been good for her. He is happy and fun loving. He makes her laugh, and he takes care of her. With him she has found a security that I could only have dreamed of for her. He keeps her safe and has promised me that he will always do that. He has my respect.

Adam, like Jill, is also good to me. He loves to come to Georgia and would move here if he could. He is profound, opinionated, strong, and gently tender. He is not a risk taker, but he does like new things. He is a Master Hair Stylist and has trained in Information Technology; he is amused that Charlaine wants to learn how to do hair too. They are a good couple. God has blessed them greatly.

In her adulthood, she has overcome cancer twice. Other health scares from childhood on have sidelined her from time to time. But, this is a woman of great strength and faith. With each trial, she has attacked it head on and with prayer and hard work, she and God have made her the winner. She will never have children. The cancer surgeries and treatments prohibited that. So, while they have no children, they have dogs and cats. These animals get the care, love, and attention that many humans never have.

Charlaine calls me every day—usually on her way home from work. We chat for a few minutes about her day and mine and whatever else comes up. She has become my best friend as well as my daughter, the answer to our prayers. No, I was not excited about adopting a little girl, but God knew more than I did what I would need. He gave me Charlaine to walk beside me when I needed someone so badly, to care, and to love me for the rest of the days of my life. I could not have asked for more. I love her dearly.

Charlaine, you are loved for the little girl you were, for the special woman you are, and the precious daughter you will always be.

FOR MY GRANDSON—JACKSON

Many of my friends commented to me, "You think you love your children, but just wait for that grandchild, and then you will know what real love is!" I laughed at them. My love for my children was so great that I could not imagine it any stronger. Plus, I really was not ready for a grandchild, I thought! One weekend, a knock at the door summoned me and there were Mark and Jill collapsing against each other with laughter. Puzzled, I wondered what in the world was wrong with them. Then, Jill handed me a gift bag in which was a little photo album entitled, "Grandma's Brag Book." Then I knew. Ready or not, here that grandchild came.

We had a great weekend planning for this baby. Just getting accustomed to the fact that there would be one was a type of magic. Some months later, we went shopping and I purchased the bed for this grandchild to be. Jill was so wonderful. Knowing that I had never been pregnant, she shared many of the details with me so that I really felt a part of this. One weekend, well into the pregnancy, Mark called her to come downstairs so that I could feel the baby moving. She allowed me to lay my hand on her tummy and feel my grandchild moving. What a marvelous experience that was.

But, it was the arrival that really made this baby special. I had teased them that they were both so clueless that they would not know when to go to the hospital. So, I was not surprised when Mark called me one night to ask what I was doing the next day. "Going to school" I replied. He said, "Well you are going to be a grandmother in the morning so you might want to miss school." He went on to tell me that they had been to the doctor for her regular appointment where she was told that she was in labor! I was shocked. Sure enough, the doctor told her to be at the hospital by 7 AM the next morning if she did not have to come in during the night. I knew it! She was in labor and they did not even know it!

Charlaine was on standby in Austin, with a ticket to come when Jill went into labor. She made plans to get the first plane out of Texas the next morning. Meeting her at the airport, we zipped down the Interstate to the hospital to walk in and see Jill being taken into the Delivery Room. The watch began.

Jill's parents, Peggy and Gerald, were there along with Charlaine and me. The four of us chatted, prayed, changed positions, and waited.

Hours went by and nothing. The entire day passed.

Charlaine would go down the hall to the room where Jill was and listen to the door every now and then. Late in the afternoon, she came running back, "I heard a cry!" She told us with her eyes sparkling and the biggest grin. Shortly, Mark came and said, "We have a son!"

In Jill's room, we saw the tiny baby in her arms. Charlaine took him and held him, cooing to him. Jill's mother and then I held him speaking to him softly. He did not respond, of course. He was so beautiful! He looked just like Mark. I could not believe it. Anyway, we had a love fest in that room—Jill's parents, Charlaine and me with the new parents and that darling baby.

I thought that I was too old to fall in love again. But in that moment, I was in love!

Eighteen years have gone by. Jackson was an adorable baby. When Jill went back to work, he would stay with me a day a week, and it was the high point. He was such a good baby. At my house he learned to say, "Mama" and to take his first steps. When he began school, I would pick him up one day a week and he was always so excited about something. This was such a joy.

When he got old enough, he would ask to come to my house which pleased me no end. We would play games, watch TV, work on the computer, and walk on the golf course. What a joy he was. . .is. I tease him now about his terrible twos lasting for too many years, but he really was not all that bad. He was a typical boy. He did not like to take a nap; and, when he spent the night, he never wanted to go to bed. I think that he just had so much that he wanted to do that he hated to give up any time at all to sleep. He loved to go to McDonalds and play in the play area. We did that a lot.

Then one morning we all got up and Jackson was grown!

Truly, it seems that way. He is a marvelous student, very good in the Humanities but a whiz at math. Writing is his real talent. Having taught writing for years, I am amazed at Jackson. When he writes an essay or a letter, whatever, it is organized as he goes along. A rough draft is not necessary. He is quite intuitive. Unlike most boys, he enjoys poetry. When Jill's father died, Jackson asked to give a part of the eulogy and read a poem he had written about his grandfather. I have a copy of it because it is AMAZING.

He played Soccer, Football, and Baseball. He prefers Baseball and is very good. He plays for his high school team. On the Little League and B teams, he has pitched and played catcher a couple of times: he loves playing third base. I think this is an homage to his hero, Chipper Janes of the Braves. Jackson is tall and well-built and very, very handsome! (No prejudice on my side at all.) He takes life seriously and loves his parents very much.

He is very good to his other grandmother and to me. He comes up to the mountains to visit me for a week at the time—now that he is old enough to drive himself, so he comes whenever he wants. He does yard work for me, moves furniture, whatever I have that needs to be done. He never complains. How do people get along without grandchildren? We always have a good time and I miss him when he leaves.

We enjoy going out to eat and have visited almost every restaurant in the area. He is so polite and has the greatest manners. I just love showing him off to my friends and to people that I do not even know!

Mark and Jill have done such a good job with him. He is polite, respectful, and a very giving person. When we are out and he meets my friends they all remark about how polite he is and how handsome! (See, I told you.) Jackson has set goals for his life since he was a little boy. Now, he is on the verge of attaining them. I could not be prouder.

When he was eight, he made his profession of faith in the Lord Jesus Christ. He was baptized with his parents and grandparents attending. He took this seriously. We talked about church and God as well as Jesus from time to time, always with great seriousness. But, I was amused when he was about ten and was visiting me. My little dog, Beauregard, was a gift from Jackson at Christmas after my other dog died. So, Jackson has an affinity for my dog and Beauregard for him. I said to Jackson, "Beauregard is just the perfect little dog." With great seriousness, Jackson turned those big brown eyes to me and said, "No, Grammie, only God is perfect!" He was so serious. I was brought up short at the maturity he was gaining.

He was about eight when my little dog was run over and killed. My heart was broken. That dog was my companion. I called Mark because I had to tell someone and cry. Bless his heart, he got off work and came to console me. I did not know it, but Jill left work and went to school and got Jackson then home and picked up her father. They drove to deep South Georgia where a Shih Tzu breeder had puppies for sale. Jackson picked out a little black male puppy for me, and they drove to my house with the little dog. I was really grieving when in walked Jackson with this tiny little black puppy in his hands and said, "Grammie, I am sorry about Schatzi, but here is a new baby for you." Well, my heart just soared. That little black dog loves Jackson like you could not believe and Jackson feels a real kinship with him. That little dog is now ten years old and is my buddy and pal. He and I walk three to five miles a day and I talk to him about everything. I do not know what I would do without that little dog, and could not do without Jackson.

Jackson makes me proud. Because Mark is adopted, he had never really known biological kin. On the day that Jackson was born, I watched Mark sit in the rocker holding Jackson in his arms and oh my, the love that was there. Jackson respects Mark and does all that he can to please him and Jill.

Jackson, I thought that I was too old to fall in love again; but, then you came along and immediately, I was in love. I cannot promise to be here and love you for all of your life; but, I can promise that I will love you for the rest of mine.

God has multiplied His goodness to me. Not only did he give me my blessed children, but he honored me with this grandchild who had stolen my heart and my love. I treasure him, knowing that the world is going to be a better place with him in it.

I begin each day of my life with a prayer of thanksgiving for all of my blessings. At the top of that list are Charlaine and Mark and their families. I know that God knows what I am going to say before I say it, but I know too, that God knows that I thank him for blessing me with my children. I thank Him that I have the relationship that I do with Charlaine and for her life and testimony. Mark has been an amazing son: he includes me in his life and I thank God for him every day. Truly, they rank right up there as a mountaintop, beloved gifts from God Himself.

My Sister, My Friend

To me you are an angel in disguise.
Full of intuition, intelligent, and wise.
Always giving and helping through
Good times and bad.
You are the best friend I've ever had.
If I had one wish it would surely be
To give you as much as you've given me.
Though I've put our relationship through some
cloudy days,
You've been my sunshine in so many ways.
Through trials and tests, right by me
You stood,
And gave me your hand whenever you could.
Thank you so much my sister, my friend
My gratitude for you has no end.
   -     Leann Stiegman, 2006

In my biological, real life, I have been blessed with three wonderful sisters, Bobbye, Sherry, and Jill who are so well described in this poem. But, through the years, there are the honorary sisters who have built on that foundation to help make me the person that I am today. I give each of you my loving thanks.

Chapter Nine

Sisters

"Friends are angels who lift us up to our feet when our own wings have trouble remembering how to fly."

In every Pastorate to which God has led us, there have been "special people"—those who *love* their Pastor family. These special people seem to understand the human side, respect the clerical side and identify with the deep needs of the one set aside. These never require, nor expect special treatment: rather, they give it! These are the ones who do not expect the Pastor knocking on their door regularly, nor do they expect him to be a mind reader. They see him as a servant of God, not as God. They do not worship him—but clearly understand that this is God's man for *this* hour. There have been others before him, and will be others after him, but for today they love, respect and serve alongside *this* one.

These are the special people who call the Pastor when a member of the flock is ill, bereaved, downtrodden, soul sick, or in need. They do not expect someone else to do it, nor do they expect some miraculous vision to inform him. These are the ones who see the Pastor as a human with human needs and emotions. These are the ones who help burp the baby, recommend a doctor, dentist, food store, auto shop, etc. In short these are the special people!

What makes these people this way, I cannot say. It must be God's way of giving His prophet, His servant, a comrade, a disciple, a hand up. Whatever the reason and the means—I am thankful that God places them—and I am grateful for the ones whom I have been privileged to know. Some of them are so special I call them my "sisters." These are the women that have befriended me especially and allowed me into their lives as a friend besides being the wife of the Pastor. These are the women that I call "sisters."

Now, I know about sisters. I am the first (I prefer not to use the term "oldest") of four girls. Simple arithmetic tells you that means that I have three sisters. I cherish them. I grew up surrounded with a type of caring and sharing that only sisters know.

When my sister, Bobbye, died, we were so stunned that we could only pray that we could stay together and that we could weather this storm. Thanks be to God, we have. The three of us are each a senior citizen now, and live a thousand miles apart. But, we are so close. We talk by phone regularly, send one another email and share our lives—the good and the not so good. For my eightieth birthday, both of them flew home and we had a party that was so very special. I suppose that it ranks up there with the greatest times of my life because we were together.

I missed them when we got out onto the church fields of the Pastorate. As a young bride, I sensed the resentment of church members when they felt that we "favored" one member, or couple. I found this unwise and never fell prey to this temptation after that realization. But I learned a far more valuable lesson. I learned that I could have the intimacy of sisterhood with these special women and still retain the church relationship. Some of these women are so special that I would commend them to the world. They are one reason there is such joy in my being a Ruth.

First, there is Mary—a true friend from whom I learned two great lessons: the first of which is how woefully inadequate I was as a wife, mother, daughter and friend; and, the second was to be aware of great and glorious gifts God sends in the understanding found in loving friends. Her relationship is precious, yet unpretentious. This is her story.

When we moved onto the field of her home church, I met Mary and her husband along with their two sons. I found her to be a SUPERPERSON. At one time, she can literally do everything! She kept an immaculate home, cooked gourmet banquets for great throngs of people, sewed lovely clothes, played the piano at church, chauffeured her boys *everywhere*, took extraordinary care of her parents, and was still obviously in love with her husband of some years. I should have hated her, but I marveled at her. Amazing is the only word descriptive of her. She was also totally honest. The "let the chips fall where they may" attitude was genuine in her. If she believed in something or someone, it was undaunted and faithful. If she did not, forget it! She reared her boys the same way and they respect her, her authority, her word, and her purposes.

After only a few months at that church, Mary announced her pregnancy. Unbeknownst to anyone, we had just applied to adopt a little girl to add to our two boys. Here was Mary glowingly talking about the little girl for which they had been praying. I remember one day especially: she came by the house and was very pregnant—huge—but glowing! She was so uncomfortable that she did not even get out of the car, but we talked through the window as I stood on the street. We laughed as we were "helping" her pick a most appropriate name for the coming daughter. I tried to sell her on Patricia, but she was having none of it. As we talked, I wanted so badly to share my own news, but could not. I bought a shower gift, lovingly lingering over little girl clothes with my own dreams. Then, Amy Sue, her daughter was born. A treasure, a love, a joy!

Two and a half months later, I looked into the face of my little girl and ironically, Amy Sue was only *three weeks older!* Mary called the afternoon we brought our baby home and her joy for us matched our own as we shared our girls' statistics. The friendship grew and in my world of anxiety and care, I found a friend with whom I could freely share my little worries and fears as well as a heavy mind. She became more than a friend, she became a "sister."

Our girls grew, played together and loved each other. Our boys played ball together and her husband was a Deacon in the church. During a depressive time for me, it was Mary who came and gave me an old fashioned sisterly scolding until I came around and straightened up! During a terrible pressing personal crisis, it was Mary who wiped my tears and from her generous heart, which God in His goodness and wisdom had endowed with a sense of understanding and power of perception, she gave me more than a friendly hand and sympathetic ear. She gave me strength to endure and miraculously, rise above. God gave her to me as a sister.

Then, we moved. I missed her and longed for her sympathetic and understanding ear, her bouncing joy to share with me. There was a new church field, and new special people, but I thought of my dear and trusted friend. We visited and wrote and I continued to love her. She invited my daughter to visit and spend the week and I trusted her more than any other person with our precious daughter.

My own sister passed away and Mary telephoned so that over the miles I could feel her love and concern giving me a new strength and reminding me anew that this union was for real and for always. Though the miles have separated us as the years go by, she remains my friend—like she was just next door. Amazingly, our daughters have remained friends. When Amy Sue was married she called upon Charlaine to do the music for her wedding. They stay in touch to this day.

Without a doubt, I know that God gave Mary to me. I wish that the world would know her as I do as a friend and as a sister. There are more wonderful women, but Mary is one of a kind and I am proud to claim her as my "special sister.

Perhaps as a young woman, the need for a best friend was keener than as the years wore on. There was Louise, about my age, childless, engrossed in building a life with her fine deacon husband and spiritually growing. She became my friend by a series of very ordinary circumstances. Putting names with faces and the right husbands with the right wives has never been one of my strong suits. Soon after moving onto this church field, we were invited to dinner by a young man. It was not unusual for me to wonder which woman would appear as his wife. When they picked us up for dinner, it was an instant friendship for the four of us.

Three hundred miles from my own family, I came to love Louise and her family in a close relationship that lasts even yet. We shared all kinds of "girl type" secrets, budget problems, family relationships, problems of homemaking and career, joys of spiritual victories, parenthood and victory. With Louise, I was first able to admit in words that being a Pastor's wife is not all smiles. From her, I learned the lesson of balancing skillfully a home, a career, a church service relationship, and still manage time for self. I found myself liking, admiring, and finally loving her. I shall always appreciate her for sharing herself so freely with me. Our fun times are among my most golden memories. I equate her with youth and its carefree path to meaningful maturity. She is high on my life of blessings, a real "sister."

The needs of a Pastor's wife go unmet for the most part. The roles of wife, mother, Sunday school teacher, confidant, counselor, housekeeper, community servant, gardener, missions teacher, seamstress, babysitter, and choir member demand, if not the best, the most one has to offer. There are times when I want to scream, "Look at me—I am me. Listen to me. I have something I want to say. Sit with me. I am alone. Hold onto me, I need to be loved."

Yet, I could not scream, nor beg, nor seek. There was no one with whom I was at liberty to be free. My husband was serving the congregation and so preoccupied that he was not aware that I might even remotely be frustrated.

I wonder that God has not long ago given up on my pleas to Him for compassionate understanding. So many times it has been God who listened to my words—unimportant though they have been. It has been God who filled me with His presence and drove away my cares and loneliness. It has been God who gently led me to paths of renewed vigor proving love. It has been God who gave me "sisters" to gently remind me that He knows my needs.

There was a time when we were new in the community and our little girl became ill. An older woman visited me quite by chance, and seeing my concern, sensing my desperation, she comforted and advised me. Calling back throughout the night, she assured me of her care and concern. She became my dear and respected friend whom I cherish right on. She "adopted" me, her own married children and grandchildren were far away. I felt the warmth of her love on many occasions and my children came to love her as a grandparent or aunt.

Another "sister" was much younger than I. Our relationship began because we had the same name and shared a burning interest in missions. As we grew closer, I became her "big" sister and came to look on her protectively as I would have my own baby sister were there not so many miles between us. We shared so much—her romantic adventures as she sought "Mr. Right," my determined efforts to understand and please the people of the church and together, our desire to know God's will. When our little girl made her appearance, this young woman made a special trip home from college to share in our joy. Three years later, our daughter was her flower girl as she wed her "Mr. Right." Truly, I was thrilled as could be with my little sister.

Annie Ruth was a "sister" too. She helped me learn to establish priorities. I will never be able to comprehend how she gave so much of herself to her family—three children, a husband. She was forever dashing around on errands concerning them, never for herself. It was constantly amazing to determine when her body ever had a chance to catch up with her soul. It did for she truly was a lovely person who gave so much love to everyone. I was blessed just to know her. Great was the blessing in being able to claim her friendship knowing that she cared about me for just me. Tragically, she was killed in an automobile accident, along with her mother, a few years ago. Truly, she was my "sister."

There is no way to enumerate all of those who have contributed in great measure to make a veritable oasis in my desert. Jamie became a mother figure. When I was hurt and dismayed, she gave me loving encouragement. Annie Ruth walked with me during the tumultuous death of my sister, holding my hand, wiping away my tears of grief with spiritual love. Sara and Harriett leaned on me for understanding and acceptance, bounding back into my life with prayerful concern just like a sister would do.

Carolyn spanned the miles to wrap me in her love when I lost my father. No one else in the whole wide world expressed themselves just for me except Carolyn. Without those moments, I would have certainly gone down for the third time. Perhaps my father's death shook my life as much or more than any single event in my adulthood. Because we had been very close and enjoyed a warm and confident relationship, I was totally unprepared to give him up. Called into responsible action as the first child, I performed the tasks that were mine with robot like precision. It was some weeks later that the impact of being without his reassuring presence in my world truly hit me. I was devastated with a terrible sensation of loneliness. Having weathered the loss of both of her parents, Carolyn sprang to my side. She alone knew the feeling, having walked recently where I now found myself. She helped me to put my life into perspective and go on from that point. I shall always remember that moment with sad thanksgiving. My sister for sure.

The list goes on: there was Gertie who stood by me when I really needed a friend and who kept in touch for years after we moved on; then, I will never forget Betty who worked a full time job and took care of her family and her mother, but always had time to chat with me and my children. On and on the list can go. Many came to me for help and wound up helping me. Others shared my burdens of home, family, and profession. Many loved me for just me—and I treasure that.

When I began to teach, I found the women of the English Department would become good friends. At the first school, I had Rita, an immigrant from Cuba who was a fabulous teacher. She worked with the Title I students and we became good friends. When she left for another position, I had Brenda with whom I teamed for almost two years. We became sisters in the best sense of the word. We were close at school and away from school. Our lives were entwined. She had taught and put her husband through law school just as I had put my husband through theology school. When she left to have her baby, I was getting ready to leave for a new church field. We still stay in contact.

But, at the next school, South Cobb, I found a group of sisters. All of the teachers in the

English Department were close. Susan was just beginning teaching and so full of life, just being around her was wonderful. Her second child was born within days of my grandson. We still are in contact.

Kitty and I were close from the beginning. She was a small woman with children in our high school. A dynamo, she never stopped. Her energy was amazing. We stayed close out of school as well as in school. We were in a night class together at a college about fifty miles away and drove back and forth together for two semesters. I taught two of her children: Charlaine taught piano to one of them. Her husband was my insurance representative. Kitty was like a kid sister. She was so peppy and energetic that she brought out the best in me. I treasure her friendship.

Then, there was Harriett. I know that there is not another woman like Harriett in this world. She was the most empathetic and sincere woman imaginable. As a teacher, she was outstanding. We had summer classes at a nearby college together and had more fun than the law allows. One class, kept us both working so hard on research and writing that had we not had each other, we may well have given up. She was really like a sister. I could tell her anything and she would understand. To this day we send one another Christmas letters. A new high school opened in our system not far from her home and she transferred there leaving a big hole in my life. I shall always treasure my time with Harriett and look at her like a sister.

There was also Celia, Sara, Jerrie, Greg, Janice, Jeanne, Doug, Jo, Robin, Janet, Gwen, and teachers from other departments like Robbie and David whose friendship I treasured and who supported me with their love and friendship when my husband passed away. With Kitty and Harriett, I sponsored the Freshman Class, and with David I sponsored the best chapter of the National Honor Society in the country! I spent thirteen years on that third floor in room 305 and they were the best years. I was allowed to spend my days with my favorite things—reading literature and writing. Moreover, I got to share that love with about 400 students per year. This was the BEST time! When I retired and moved away, I really felt that I had lost something special from these my sisters.

What I learned from these women were that to apologize take bravery, to forgive comes from strength, and to forget breeds great happiness. Many times we sat in the English Office commiserating over one thing or another; always, they took the time to listen and to understand. They taught me to handle each day by meeting it head on, then moving on to the next day. We called ourselves "The Ivory Tower." For thirteen years we met in September to undertake to make a difference in the lives of the students who would populate our classrooms; then, we parted in June after reviewing our successes and our failures, secure in the knowledge that we had done our best. Then we began again the next September. Perhaps the best lesson that I learned from them is that "To teach is to learn twice." A teacher takes the hand of a student in the effort to make his life more meaningful by planting seeds that bear fruit in the years that follow, never giving up.

Not all of the ladies in a church or group qualify as "sisters." Most of them are extraordinarily compassionate and delightfully friendly. I have had grandmotherly ladies come to bring homemade jelly and talk; motherly types who bring fresh vegetables and talk; those my age who come with a pie to talk; and, young ladies who come with their problems to talk. I love them all and treasure the fact that they love and trust me. "Sisters" are rare. Equally as rare are those who cause great affliction to Ruth by words and deeds.

Women can be very cliquish, joining ranks at surprising times. Jokes are plentiful regarding gossiping women, picky women and unhappy women. It has been my happy lot to encounter so many fine women that my life has been made richer because of them. I count it a privilege to call them friends. Many have looked on me with pity because of my role in life. Others have treated me with disdain or tolerance. I have been enthroned as special and cast out in contempt. By and large, I have been accepted and my lot in life has been enhanced by those with whom I have served.

When Mark married Jill, her mother, Peggy, became my good friend. When I moved to Macon, we really became friends. Because we share a grandson that makes us really close. When we lived in the same town, we really shared Jackson. She would keep him for a couple of days a week, and then I would keep him for a day or two. Her husband would join Jill, Mark, Jackson, and me for dinner and we would have little outings together. Peggy and I would talk by phone and when we were visiting about everything. We share secrets and our hopes and dreams for Jackson still. She has been to the mountains to visit me and we sat on the porch and enjoyed our time together. She has sisters as do I, but to me, she is a sister as well. I truly love her.

When Charlaine married Adam, I met Cynthia, Adam's mother. What a fine lady she is. She is elegant, refined, and lovely in looks and in spirit. I was so delighted to find that she had a superior sense of humor and shared my love of books and our children. At their wedding, she looked at her son with so much love and pride that I knew in that moment that she and I would be friends—more like sisters. She lives over a thousand miles from me, but we stay in touch by Facebook and through our children. If she were closer in residence, I know that we would enjoy lots of time together. As it is, we support one another with our love and our prayers. She is a trauma nurse and travels the world with Doctors without Borders training medical personnel in third world countries in burn treatment. A wonderful Christian, she begins her days with prayer and carries her close relationship with God with her throughout her day. Our world is a better place because of Cynthia, my sister friend.

Upon the death of my husband, I became a "regular church member." I must admit that letting go of my "pastor's wife" status was not automatic or easy. But, there was a bit of release as well. This became an adventure to me. I stayed a member of the local church in the community where I bought a house for several years. The folks there had known me as a

Pastor's wife, so I did not quite have the "regular" status. But, when I retired, moved to my mountain home and united with the church there, things changed. Nobody kept up with my attendance at any of the church meetings. I was not treated any differently at all. This was so different. But, the most outstanding difference was that I could feel free to have friends with whom I shared lunch, a telephone conversation, a visit over the fence, or swap pieces of pie.

One of these women who has become just like my sister is Georgia. We are backdoor neighbors, members of the same Sunday school class, and friends. We keep up with one another. If I do not see her lights come on, I check on her, and she does the same. When she goes out of town, I keep an eye on her house and she returns the favor. We chat on the phone regularly about absolutely nothing and about everything in the world. While we do think a great deal alike, we also have differences that do not bother us. In fact, it "spices" up our conversations. We laugh and giggle like high schoolers over the slightest thing. When I see her number come up on caller ID, I smile. I know that the day has just gotten brighter. When I am lonely or heartsick, I can call her and know that I will come away feeling so much better. We don't necessarily talk about my problem or loneliness, we just talk. She and I are close in age, both widows. She is from

Florida and shares her experiences there and in her native Pennsylvania. We converse about money, TV programs, the weather, men, and our family. We always have the best time together. We joke about the fact that if the world would just listen to us, we could solve all of its problems. We do have opinions that are valuable! I know that God put her in that house to be my sister. How thankful I am to know that she is there. She is not shy, she is interesting, she is a Christian and represents Christ in all that she says and does. She has no enemies. I know that I am a better person for knowing her; and, I am totally confident that she is my "sister," a blessing I acknowledge every day. Truly, I love her. Paul wrote in I Corinthians 13, "And now abided faith, hope, and love: but the greatest of these is love." That is what Georgia is to me, a gift of love. She has the spirit of faith, the heart of kindness, the character of beauty: she is an amazing woman.

Another joy in this newfound widowhood of mine is Marjorie who lives with her husband down the road from me. They live in Florida half of the year and here the other half. When they are here, Marjorie and I have the best times. We laugh; we commiserate on health problems, talk about our children, and family. Sometimes we get deep into a conversation and the time is just gone. A reader like me, we share our feelings about books—recommending the good ones and dissing the not so good ones. Her husband is a big baseball fan, so we share that in common. As well, we discuss the problems of our country and come up with GREAT solutions. My little dog adores them. Every time that they go out to eat, they bring him a doggie bag. He knows their car and when it goes by without stopping, he is so pitiful. When they stop, he is beside himself to see what they have brought to him. She says that they are his "meals on wheels." They are wonderful neighbors and friends. She is a Methodist and a wonderful Christian, so we share the love of God as well. In Marjorie I have found a "sister" who is warm and friendly, but also faithful, loyal, and good. When they are in Florida, we talk by phone which keeps our relationship fresh. God gives His children wonderful gifts, too numerous to count. But, when He gives us a good friend who becomes a "sister" we know how much He loves us. Marjorie has proven that for me. Truly, "the greatest of these is love."

Perhaps the greatest lesson that I have learned from Marjorie is that life should not be a journey to the grave with the intention of arriving safely in a well preserved body, but rather a "skid in sideways, with chocolate in one hand and a good book in the other, body thoroughly worn out and screaming. . . 'Woo Hoo, What a ride!'" That is the powerful friend that she is! I love her.

Sara is younger than me and moved in next door for almost two years. I found her to be exceptional. When I was ill, she came every day to check on me. She washed my clothes and my dishes, made my bed, folded my underwear, and sat with me. When I was well, we visited and talked, laughed, and even cried a little bit. She would go out to walk with her little dog and come by here so that the dogs could play. We would have the greatest visits. When her granddaughter was born, she shared the baby with me and made me feel like an honorary grandmother. She still telephones me regularly to see how I am doing and we talk about the world and all that is in it. She came into my life at a time when I needed someone. We visited for a little time each day for the longest time. Then, she fell in love and moved away. We still talk and we are still the best of friends. I told her that I was very jealous—and I really was! Truly, I count her a "sister." God always takes care of our needs, often before we are aware of them. He brought Sara into my life and she has become like a "sister" to me. I thank God for her.

All of the members of the Esther Sunday School class have been like my best friends. I love them dearly. We are a sisterhood. We share blessings and prayers. We laugh and have a good time with one another. When we are together on Sunday mornings, the chatter is like a gaggle of geese. We study God's word together and are not afraid to ask questions or to say what we believe. We have a very strong prayer chain. When one of us is troubled, ill, or in need in any way, all of us are there. We activate our prayer chain and God seems to listen, for He has answered our prayers so many times. When God put this group of women together, He chose from the cream of the crop. They are wonderful. They are my "sisters." I love each of them dearly and am so grateful that God brought me to this place at this time so that I could get to know them.

Laverne is a woman that everyone needs for a best friend/sister. She is a rock. Nothing upsets her. She is quiet and unassuming as she goes about doing God's will. To me she represents all that is good and right in a world trying to go wrong. I value her and her presence in my life has certainly become essential.

Then there is Teresa! I am not sure that I can put into words what she is like. She is so full of life that feeling sad or down when around her is impossible. Her smile is like sunshine and her laughter had to be the spawn of angels. She is kind to the ultimate and a child of God. Everything that she does has an element of spice in it. She is the pal that every woman needs at this time in life. I treasure her friendship.

There are two other women that I put into this category in a slightly different relationship: they are my daughter, Charlaine, and my daughter in law, Jill.

Charlaine is the one female in this world whom I know that I can call on for physical, mental, and emotional support at anytime and anywhere. Yes, she is my child, but our relationship goes beyond that. Life has not been a piece of cake for Charlaine, she has had her share of problems; but, the way that she meets them is amazing. She will react emotionally for a bit and then she begins to seek a way to solve the problem or overcome the difficulty. She is strong in every way. She is the quintessential musician. Her ability at the piano and with her voice is absolutely amazing. Trained as a concert pianist, she was an outstanding student. Yet, when she finished her Master's degree she elected NOT to pursue music as a career because of the strain on her nerves—stage fright. She loved playing, but was wise enough to find another way to make a career. That took strength and courage beyond what many of us possess. We share experiences, ideas, and dreams that we can share with no one else. Her husband does not resent our closeness for he is a part of it. Charlaine is attracted to needy situations and people with needs. Not afraid to get involved, she has some unique solutions at times. She is kind, loving, beautiful, sincere and loyal to the bone. I treasure her in ways there are no words to express and I thank God for her every single day.

Jill came into my life as Mark's girlfriend and is now his wife and the mother of my grandson. She is everything that I, myself, would want to be. She is a tiny young woman who wears her clothes so well: she has exquisite taste in clothes, home making, friends, and everything else. Her ability to be strong regardless has been shown so many times. She is vivacious and attacks life with some sort of zeal that is unique for her. Living with two men—Jackson and Mark—who are big and strong when she is so tiny, she still exerts her will and lets them know who is really the boss! She is great in our family. She does not argue, but listens to all sides, and if pushed will give her opinion. She is so intelligent. I am continually impressed with her drive and her wisdom. When Mike needed emotional strength she was there for him: she loved him but she was quick to redirect his life when he needed it. To me, she has been a godsend. She loves my son and has made a wonderful mother—that alone makes her special. But, if she was not with Mark, I would still love her and admire her strength and the way she attacks life with dignity; and, I would want her for my friend. My life would not be as complete. Truly, I love her.

So, I must include these two with the amazing women in my life. How fortunate I am that God brought them to me.

Years ago in grade school, a classmate wrote a poem in my autograph book that perhaps sums up the whole affair:

"There are gold ships and silver ships.

But there are no ships like friendships."

These are the people who have taught me to praise God in my happy moment, to seek God in the difficult times, to trust God in my quiet times, and to thank God in every moment. I am thankful for them as they parade through my heart, mind, and soul.

"How natural it is that I should feel as I do about you, for you have a very special place in my heart. We have shared together the blessings of God . . . We are in this . . . together."

\-   Phil. 1:7, 8, 30 TLB

Chapter Ten

If I had it to do over. . .

I n any life situation, there are positives and negatives. Being a Pastor's wife has very definite minuses . . . but, there are so many pluses to offset or diminish the minuses. What really is necessary is a continual counting of one's blessings. In so doing, those blessings are magnified. When looking at the woman who is the Pastor's wife, one must consider her first as a human being— fallible but ready and eager to rise above that— but also a spiritual being who has an enlightened view of the church and its work in the world of today. She should be respected and understood, befriended and loved. She is a wife, a mother, and a helpmeet. She wants to understand and needs support.

As I look back on the decades of my life, I think that my major minus has been the lack of real roots. Having childhood memories of grandparents, cousins, long term neighbors and only one school system, I feel that my own children were deprived of that. At times I would fantasize about putting down permanent roots, buying a house, and growing old in one place— to me, this spells security. Yet, I know deep down that roots do not necessarily stay in place or in time: indeed, our roots have been in our moving and following God's leading. When I allow myself to look inward, I recognize that in the midst of the changes moving has brought real roots which have grown deeper and wider that are not based on blood or place, but on struggles shared, passion, pain and growth. Some time on dark, dreary winter mornings, I would yearn for that sense of place. But on bright, happy days, I felt blessed. My children are more well-rounded because of their experiences, more adept at meeting new people, better adjusted, and certainly, totally unaware of anything that I fear they have missed.

Another of my minuses is a lack of privacy. I am by nature a very private person. I have been keenly aware that truly we have lived with glass walls. Our home was always open to whomever needed us at any time. This is illustrated by the night a young couple from a distant town came to our home to be married one Saturday afternoon. Michael was a toddler then and looked totally unimpressed. After the ceremony in our lovely and rarely used living room, I found a half eaten apple on the end table. Then, after midnight on a cold winter Saturday night, another couple, this one not quite so young, came and got us out of bed so that they could be married. I became their Matron of Honor in my old green fleece bathrobe, and Michel was their best man in jeans, a tee shirt and barefoot.

As the children grew, the number of visitors multiplied. No longer just troubled church members or curious ladies or perhaps children with their cars and blocks, now we had all of those plus teenagers who wanted to talk about personal or family problems, friends of our children who responded to their invitation to come and "talk to my folks about it." Some came to listen to loud noise that they call music. I found myself holding constant open house with a chronically empty refrigerator. After I began to teach, they would bring their friends home for help with homework. I shall never forget when Mike brought one of the football players home with him telling me that unless the boy could turn in a paper that passed, he would be kicked off of the team. I did not personally know the boy but agreed to look at his paper and make suggestions. I was amazed at the punctuation and asked him what rule he was using. He replied, "Rule? I don't know a rule. I just put in "those little jobbers" (he meant commas) every once in a while so it would look good!" As an English teacher, I was horrified. We had a little lesson at the kitchen table.

There was never a time to lock the door and have a nap, read a whole chapter in a book, or even argue with my husband. But, we survived. We had "instant belonging" in a community where we served. Clubs accepted us immediately; the busiest beauty shop made room for me; merchants showed me quality merchandise from the back room, often at a discount.

I missed being close to my family to share my children with them. But, I learned that as a Ruth, I had to totally depend on God to walk with Him daily and the difficult times became better. When my mother passed away, there were those there to hold my hand and help me through the days that followed as I traveled back and forth to settle her estate. When my tears of fatigue and loneliness would fall, I would then experience the sweetness of relief at the strength and comfort that washed over me in knowing that in the center of God's will there is peace.

There are people who ask me if I knew what I was getting into when I married Charles. Honestly, I thought I did, but there was so much more. There was more responsibility, sharing, heartbreak, sorrow, joy, happiness, satisfaction, and fulfillment. I chose this life because I loved him and I loved God. Together we have found the absolute exultation of knowing what it is like to be in the center of God's will. So, my answer is without a doubt, YES, if I had it to do again, I would do the same thing. I would not want to miss knowing the people in the churches we served; I would not want to be without my children just like they are; and, I would not want to miss learning how to completely depend on God.

I was disappointed when my husband announced he only wanted to Pastor small town churches. I envisioned large city churches with great expensive programs to meet the needs of their people. But, I have found that God calls different men to different areas. We served in rural Pastorates, small towns, and cities. Maturity taught me that being where God wants us to be is the answer.

Then the moment came for which I had not prepared at all.

Crossing the Bar

Sunset and evening star
And one clear call for me!
And may there be no moaning of the bar,
When I put out to sea,

But such a tide as moving seems asleep,
Too full for sound and foam,
When that which drew from out the boundless
deep
Turns again home.

Twilight and evening bell,
And after that the dark!
And may there be no sadness of farewell,
When I embark;

For though from out our bourne of Time and
Place
The flood may bear me far,
I hope to see my Pilot face to face
When I have crossed the bar.

-        Alfred Lord Tenneyson, 1889

"For now we see through a glass, darkly, but then
face to face: now I know in part; but then shall I
know even as also I am known." I Corinthians
13:12 KJV

Chapter Eleven

Until death do us part

As I grew older, I would think about the future and realize that things would not always be the same. I lost my sister, my father, and my mother. I had known that Mother and Daddy would likely precede me in death. I was not prepared for my sister to die before me. But, when Charles and I married, we promised "until death do us part."

That happened.

Life was moving along as usual. Michael was working at the prison; Mark was working at the college, Charlaine was a college senior. I was teaching and loving my life. The church where he pastored was very sound. There were elements of growth and signs of the love these people shared. God lived there.

Summer came.

As Charles had done for several years, he went to Brazil on a Missions trip with several other ministers from the Southern Baptist Convention. I took him to the airport and went home to enjoy my vacation from school. He would be gone two weeks. After a week, I got a call from Brazil and one of the other ministers to tell me that Charles was coming home and when to meet his flight. Puzzled, I prepared to go to the airport. At that time, going all of the way to the gate to meet the plane was permitted—it was before 9/11 and all of the security changes.

Seeing him come down the ramp from the plane I noticed that he was absolutely gray. Still not comfortable with him coming home early, I figured that he was tired. Quickly, I saw that he had a terrible cough; but, as was his habit, he refused to go to the doctor. (He was never sick!) He felt that he just had a cold from "riding back to the hotel from the revival meeting in an open bus when wet with perspiration." But, on Sunday night, he could not finish his message because he was coughing so badly. This forced him to give in and go to the doctor the next day.

Preplanning had started for school and I was there all day. When I came home, he told me that the doctor had diagnosed him with bronchitis and given him medicine including some cough syrup and had done an x-ray.

The next day, he got a call to bring me and come to the doctor's office. I left school and met him at home and we drove there. The doctor told us that the x-ray showed something—tuberculosis, a tumor, or cancer! This was not a simple case of bronchitis!

Talk about sitting up and taking notice.

We did.

The next day, I took the day off and we went to the hospital for tests. I waited and waited and waited. At last, a nurse came out and told me that Charles was dressing and that I should find an Oncologist. The diagnosis was that he had about a year to live. My world slowed down.

I knew what that meant. Cancer.

We set up appointments with the Oncologist for the next week. We were told that he had cancer but that they could not find the mother tumor and wanted to hospitalize him for further testing. He was getting sicker by the day. I learned that while he was in Brazil he had hemorrhaged which is why he came home early. Michael was at home with him during the day and I was there at night. During those tests, they found that the mother tumor was in his kidneys and had manifested itself in his lungs. They gave him six months to live.

Chemo was prescribed and began within a week. For his first treatment, Michael took him and reported that afternoon that Charles was so very sick. Sure enough, when I got home, he was beyond anything I had ever encountered. The oncologist changed his prediction to three months to live.

Charles wanted to make one more trip to the mountains. So, after I got in from school we drove up there. I knew that he was a sick man, but I do not think that I had let myself understand how sick he was. We stopped for him to go to the bathroom and as he got out of the car and walked across the parking lot, he could barely walk. My heart just broke for him. We got to the house and I got things opened up and the heat going. He could only sit in the recliner. He could eat no dinner. That night he hemorrhaged again and I had to call the ambulance to get him to this hospital. The doctor there told me to call my children, that he might not make the night.

With the children there the next day, the doctor told us that the little hospital there could not handle anything this serious. Because we were friends, he went further and told me that he did not think that Charles would make it until Halloween! We had to take him back home to the hospital there. The ambulance loaded him up and we began the 150 mile trip home. Mark drove my car and I rode with him. Jill, Mark's girlfriend, brought Michael who had ridden up with Charlaine, and she came alone. We made a caravan, none of us knowing what to expect. After we crossed the mountains and got on the four lane highway, suddenly, the ambulance flashed its lights, sped up and took off. I looked at Mark and he looked at me and hit the gas. When we got to the hospital, they were unloading Charles into the Emergency Room and told us that they had almost lost him on the road. The doctor met us here and grimly told us that this was the beginning of the end.

I began the week by going to school during the day and staying at the hospital at night. Charles was fading fast. Finally, my principal came to the hospital and told me to forget coming into school, to stay with him that my classes would be covered. So, I moved into the hospital room.

We spent long hours talking about our lives and how God had used us. We remembered good times and good people. We talked about the children and what a joy they had been. We talked about their futures and what we wanted for them. I read the newspaper to him. He would give me a passage of scripture and I would look it up and read it to him. We did our devotionals every day. We prayed together, and as he slept, I prayed like I had never prayed before.

Charles planned his funeral: my heart broke.

Our church people came to the hospital and brought me food and comfort. They prayed for him and with him. They cared for me and for our children who were all at our house. Other friends from previous churches heard the news and came to pray with us. There was a sense of peace in that room that I cannot explain.

On Sunday, his family came to sit with him and suggested that I take a break. I went out into the waiting room where there was a little private alcove. I curled up there to pray and to cry and fell asleep. I dreamed that someone came into the room and told me that everything was going to be alright, that I should stop my weeping and rejoice that God was in control and all would be well. An angel came all dressed in filmy blue and white and took me into her arms to assure me that all was well. I awoke feeling refreshed, secure, and confident and went back to the room where Charles was coughing so badly and had turned absolutely gray again. His mother had summoned the nurses.

The next few days were very hard. He was deteriorating rapidly. We had to stop the visitors.

I stayed awake all night. His pain was so intense that they were giving him straight morphine which made him have hallucinations. He would preach, talk to various people and talk about things that had happened years ago. My heart was in tiny pieces and my soul was in so much pain. I could only hold his hand and pray.

Thursday morning, I realized that his breathing was more labored and that his color was worse. He was totally quiet. I had spent the night beside his bed holding his hand and by dawn feared the worst. I called for the nurse who told me that I should call the children that he was going down rapidly. The doctor came and insisted that they be called immediately.

They came.

Michael got there first and his face contorted at the sight of his father in such pain. The cancer had reached his brain. He was in and out of consciousness.

Charlaine got there next and took his hand. He opened his eyes. I believe that he recognized her, because he smiled.

Mark came in last: he had to drive from the northern part of the city in the morning traffic. Amazingly, he had made it with no delays at all.

He took his father's hand causing Charles to open his eyes and squeeze his hand.

The nurse came in and checked his oxygen and morphine and told us that we should talk to him. She explained that hearing is the last sense to go. So, we did.

We gathered as a family and we told him about what was going on with each of us.

We prayed and we talked about the wonderful things that God had done for him and with him.

Just before 11 AM, he breathed his last.

Charles was gone.

Six weeks from the time that he returned from Brazil, God had called him home to heaven.

But, we were left here. There are no words to describe that feeling. None.

That afternoon we made the arrangements. I took a shower and got into my bed knowing that I should sleep, but could not. But, I stayed there playing all of this over and over in my mind. Charles's brother came by and visited for a bit. He was grieving too. The next day we were in a daze. The phone rang and people came with food but there was a sense of unreality.

How does one handle this?

At the funeral, the church was packed. The Pastor's Association served as honorary pall bearers and filled several pews as did the deacons of our church. There were people there from every church he had ever served: people that he had baptized decades ago, couples he had married years ago. Many of my students came as did the friends of our children. There was no room to even stand. The church was full. Men of the ministry with whom Charles had grown up did the music and eulogy. A senior Pastor of the Convention did the message. Charlaine played the piano, her father's favorite song. Then there was the long trip to the cemetery where he was laid to rest beside his brother who had been killed in World War II, and his father whose funeral Charles had done himself.

And it was over.

A thirty five year marriage ended that day; the dedicated ministry of one man ended; three people lost their father. But wait! Is that true? My vow was until death do us part and I am still here—married. Charles's ministry goes on in the lives of the people he touched, baptized, married, and counseled: the churches where he served have programs that he instituted, building programs, missions emphasis—so his ministry goes on. Our children have the lessons learned from him, the wise advice he gave them, the example that he set for them. His life will continue in them.

So, my sadness was mollified somewhat; but, I had to determine what was next for me with God's help. A part of me remained stunned for a very long time. Losing what had been a part of me left me without a partner to blaze the trail or walk by my side. Having given myself to God, I knew that He would not desert me at this time, and He did not. With each step that I have taken, I have felt His presence in my life in a whole new way. At times the road has been a bit rocky, but tackling it was not a question: God put it before me and my following it was His will.

A new chapter in my life began.

". . . Lo, I am with you always, even to the end of the world."

-     Matthew 28:30 KJV

"As the marsh hen builds on the watery sod, Behold, I will build me a nest on the greatness of God. I will fly in the greatness of God as the marsh hen flies in the freedom that fills all the space 'twixt the marsh and the skies. By so many roots as the marsh grass sends in the sod I will heartily lay me a hold on the greatness of God."

-     From "The Marshes of Glynn," Sidney Lanier

"Peace I leave with you. My peace I give unto you: not as the world giveth, give I unto you. Let not your heart be troubled, neither be afraid"

-     I John 14:27.

Chapter Twelve

And, now what?

When doctors first told us that Charles was terminal, I began to wonder what in the world we would do. Remember, we had always lived in Pastoriums—homes owned by the church that we were serving. The furniture and appliances were ours, all of the dishes and linens were ours, but where would we put them? Common sense told me early that another person would be coming along to take that Pastorate and need that house. My question was how long it would take me to make the changes that had to be made. Never was that more obvious than the day after Charles's funeral.

Once, when Charles was lucid, he told Charlaine to ride around the town and pick out a house that would suit our needs. She took that task seriously and two days later came back to tell us that she had found it. She described it beautifully: there was a study in one of the front rooms where we could move Charles's hospital bed and have it by the windows so that he could look out at the gardens and trees, she told us. Also, this room had its own bathroom which she thought was perfect for him. I think that there were four or five bedrooms, a living room, a family room, a huge kitchen, breakfast room, four bathrooms, two large decks, and a beautifully landscaped yard. I had never bought a house, but it did not take long for me to determine that this was WAY beyond what we could afford. But, at Charles's insistence, I went and looked at it. Yes, it was amazing: so, was the price. I hated to disappoint her, but we would not be living there.

Lying awake at night and replaying my life over and over, I now realized all over again how God had been taking care of me. He had moved us to a church close enough to a university that I could commute and get a degree so that I could teach and earn a living. Had that opportunity not been afforded to me, there would have been no way that I could have supported us when he was gone. Then, God had moved us to the present church adjacent to the best school system in the State of Georgia where the pay was higher and the standards high as well. As soon as we had moved, I had applied for a position but was told that there were "stacks" of applicants waiting ahead of mine. But, by chance, a member of this new church "knew someone" who worked in the offices of the system and who saw to it that my application was moved up to the very top. I was interviewed and given a job close to my home using gifted certification that I had acquired in addition to my degree simply because the classes were offered at a convenient time for me. God does work in mysterious ways.

Working in that system for four years, I had continued going to school at night and obtained my Master's degree which had given me a generous raise in pay. We had saved some of that money while helping our children at the same time. But now, I realized that I could afford to buy a house and pay the bills for Charlaine and for me as well as help the boys get situated in their new lives as well.

We did get busy looking for a house. My principal had assured me that my job was safe and there for years to come. So, I made up my mind that God had led us here and here we would stay. We looked at houses of every type. Once we came up with a price we could afford and what we needed we found many houses. Mark came and drove around with us looking at houses of all kinds.

But, there was one that I loved—in a very convenient, safe, and beautiful neighborhood. The house was brand new and very well decorated. All we had to do was move in. Armed with a brochure about the house and the cost, with my financial records, and prayers galore, I went to the bank. A very kind man sat with me and looked at all of my information, our tax return, my finances, and what I could look forward to in the coming years as far as income was concerned. He looked at the materials on the house I wanted and without any problem granted me a loan to buy the house. While he got the paper work started, I got into my car and put my head on the steering wheel to pray a prayer of thanksgiving.

God had come through for me again.

Then, the day came for me to sign the loan papers. This time, when it was done and I took the keys and got into my car, I had to weep and thank God for giving me a future and a way to keep my family together. We would not be pushed out into something that was not appropriate.

I did not take one of my children with me.

Somehow I knew that God and I could handle this. When I left the bank, I went straight to the house. I unlocked the front door and walked into the foyer and just stood there.

This was MY house. My own home.

A place where my children and I would find safety and security. Ironically, it was not a tent, nor any of the other things I had feared we would have to occupy. There were three bedrooms—one for me downstairs, with its own bath; upstairs there were two big bedrooms, each with its own bath: one for the boys and one for Charlaine. I had a dream kitchen and my own fireplace. There was a garage for my car, and a laundry room with its own door. I had a pantry. There was a deck that opened off of the breakfast room and the den, where I could sit and see nothing by trees. No, this was more than a house; it was a home, a place of serenity for us after the storm we had endured. How great was God to find this for us?

The church was wonderful to us. The deacons asked me to meet with them where they told me that they were going to pay Charles's salary to us for three months which gave us the funds to take care of the medical and funeral bills. They asked me if I thought that we could be out of the house in three months: I assured them that we would be out before that. When I shared my news about the house, they were thrilled for us. Their prayers were answered too. These men were so eager to be sure that we would be alright that my heart just overflowed. I had to realize anew that when God wants you in a place, it is for YOUR wellbeing as well as what you can help the people to do. I learned that lesson. The church at Union Grove in Lithia Springs treated us with so much respect and love. I knew that it came straight from God.

So, we moved into our house by Christmas. All of the children came home and we had our first Christmas without Charles. Sad? Yes, we were. But, at the same time we were thankful that we had not had to watch him suffer for an extended period. The six weeks he had been sick had hurt to the core of our being. We were not only sad, we were numb. Accepting so many changes in such a short time had caused all of us to be unsettled, wary, and a bit insecure. We went to the Christmas Eve Candlelight Service at the church where Charlaine had accepted a position in the Music Ministry. How close we were to God that night! All of us.

The children went back to their school and jobs, and I went back to mine. But, there was a difference. Suddenly, I was in charge of everything. Now, I had never lived alone, been responsible for the bills, house payment, none of that. I went from my father's house to Charles's house. Now, I was the "go to gal." I had to make a budget and determine how we would live from now on. I can tell you that only the grace of God got me through that. The learning curve was steep.

My students were so wonderful to me when I returned to school. They had a brunch—meaning that each of them had brought some wonderful breakfast food and decorated my classroom. This was a surprise which thrilled them. They hugged me, gave me cards, and were sympathetic. The principal dropped in as well as the other English teachers. This gave me a little boost to get me started back to normal.

A woman is one thing when she is wife and mother—even when she is a Pastor's wife and following in the steps of Ruth. But, when she is widowed, she moves into another bracket altogether. My friends looked at me differently: they had their husbands and were self-conscious around me. The church looked at me differently, like I needed to know about how to keep things moving. My children looked at me differently, like "Are we going to have to put you in a home? Take care of you? What?" I looked at myself differently; I knew that if life was going to go on, I had to step up. But, God looked at me just the same—His child in whom He had confidence and whom He loved. My prayer life was much improved, especially when the dry cleaning needed to be picked up, the bills came, groceries needed buying, and a hundred other things needed attention. Very calmly, with God's help beside me constantly, I took it one step at a time. We made it!

One year later, Mark got married. I knew it was coming, but when it did, I could only think of how much he needed his father at that time. But, they planned their wedding and their life after and it all went off like clockwork. Again, people from former church fields showed up to support us with their presence and their love.

God came through for us again.

Then Charlaine was offered a position in Austin, Texas. She went out there alone to look for an apartment. I knew that she would turn it down: she had never even lived in a dorm. She would not go a thousand miles away. But, she did. My heart was broken. For the first time in my life I was alone. Just my little dog and me. I knew that I could not do this. But, I did. I am even now totally shocked at how smoothly our lives worked out. People have asked me how we did it. I tell them: "We didn't. God did."

Then, along came Jackson, Mark and Jill's son, my grandson seven years later. I was not ready to be a grandmother—I thought. But, the day that he was born, Charlaine flew home from Texas to be there for Mark and Jill and to greet her nephew. We sat with Jill's parents for the whole day awaiting the arrival of this baby. When he finally came, he was beautiful. I was in love from that moment onward. I had prayed for a safe delivery for Jill—she is so tiny and had worked so hard to keep her body in perfect shape for the baby's health (even gave up coffee which she loved!). I prayed for the baby to be healthy and ready for us to love. I knew he was a boy. I saw the ultrasound. I did not tell them, because they elected not to know. But, I knew. Sure enough, at eight pounds and 20.5 inches long he entered the world about 4 PM that day. Oh my, what a beautiful baby he was. I held him and looked into a little face just like Mark's. I was so thankful when I looked at Mark as he held his son. My heart almost burst—I was sad that Charles was not there but knew that he was watching over us. God had him in the right place.

Then, five years later Charlaine got married. Jackson was the Ring Bearer and was adorable in his little tux. Mark gave her away. She was a beautiful bride and on that day there was the promise of GREAT things ahead. They stood beside the Christmas tree and you could just see God and her father smiling down on them. One of her pictures of the wedding show her sitting on Santa's lap. She did not need anything from Santa. God had given her the answer to her prayers. I could only offer up prayers of gratitude.

Five years later, with things going so well, we were shaken to our core when Michael died. My sister had taken her life before my father died, some thirty years before. That was a shock that

still resonates within my heart. My parents'
deaths hurt me deeply, but I had known all of my
life that I would have to tell them goodbye. But,
my child? No, never in all of my life had I
contemplated giving one of my children up to the
grave. The night that I got the call, a piece of my
heart just broke off, never to be replaced. To this
day, I am still shocked that he is gone. Mark,
Jackson, and Jill, Charlaine and Adam, and I
bade him goodbye at a celebration of his life.
My sister, Sherry, with her daughters, my nieces,
came. Joel, Charles's brother came with his
wife. Mike's friends were there and again,
people from our former churches. God kept us
strong.

There are so many times when I feel him close
by me. Mike and I were very close. He never
married, so we spent a great deal of time
together. We talked regularly by phone even
"watched" football games together—him in
South Georgia and me in North Georgia. I miss
him with all of my heart and soul. But, I know
beyond a doubt that God knew what He was
doing and that Mike is so much better off, and
still in our hearts.

Charles has been gone for twenty six years. So
much has happened, so many changes in the
world and in our lives. He must be amazed in
heaven that we have managed to handle it all.
The reason we have is that in our ministry we

learned to depend on God, to seek out the center of His will and follow Him wherever He led. That is how I became a Ruth. My commitment was to go where God led us, worship together, and love His people, for the rest of my life. His death changed the geography of that, but I am still doing those things as are my children.

Now retired from teaching—both high school and college—I have returned to the place where I was born, Hiawassee, Georgia. As a little girl, I would visit my grandparents here during the summer. One year, when I was preparing to go back home with Mother and Daddy and back to school, I walked with my Grandfather Sutton to the mail box and looked again at the beautiful Blue Ridge Mountains and told him that when I was "big" I was going to live here full time and never have to go back to the city. Because he was a realist and he loved me, he gave me a hug and said, "Sure, you will, Patsy, sure you will!" As the years went on, I would remind my family of that goal in my life and no one believed it. Yet, here I am. I have everything that I need:

Dr. Joey takes care of my eyes, reprimands me when I do not do the things that I should do to assure my eye health, and commends me when I do obey. He is a definite positive in this new life of mine.

The wonderful people at Chatuge Family Care have given me superb medical care even when I was only here part time. Drs. Johnson and Brendt have seen me through some really hard times, along with my pulmonary guy, Dr. Brown in Gainesville and my heart guy at Emory, Dr. Lutz. This team has guarded my health, found the proper treatments, and given me some really hard lectures when appropriate.

The great folks at Rite Aid have also been guardians of my health. Al Strickland and his team have kept me going and given me advice, support, and lectures as needed. I truly owe them a great debt of gratitude.

Then, the joy of home ownership, so many little things need attention, so "Who you gonna call?" I call Paul, the wonderful man who keeps my home in shape and answers all of my calls even for the dumbest things. He is a life saver and so gallant!

In addition, I have a great super market, shops, restaurants, and fast food places which add to my comfort here.

My church, McConnell Memorial Baptist Church has been like a lighthouse for me. From that church I have received comfort, spiritual guidance, and the opportunity to teach a Sunday

312

school class of Senior Ladies where I have found my joy.

I do miss my family, however. I know that each of them is where (s)he should be, but there are days when I really just need to touch them, receive a hug, and sit down with them. I do love them so very much.

Today Mark and Jill both are Computer Scientists as civilian employees of the U. S. Air Force in Macon, Georgia; Jackson is graduating from high school and already accepted at Mercer University (his grandfather, father, mother and aunt all went there, and I taught there). Charlaine is Archivist for the Lyndon B. Johnson Presidential Library in Austin, Texas, and Adam has his own businesses there. I live in the mountains I always loved so much, high up on a mountain top, with my little dog, Beauregard. I teach my Sunday School Class of senior ladies, work with the Women's Missionary Union in my church, and am a member of Eastern Star and Retired Teachers. My time is my own. My life is in God's hands.

Lonely? Yes, there are times when this emotion creeps up on me. But, I am not alone—never alone. I have my memories, my plans, my tasks, and my dreams. However, the presence of God in all that I say and do gives me the confidence to awaken to each new morning with joy. Life is good

Charles's mother passed away a few years ago after grieving his loss so profoundly. The brother in law he had loved for so many years passed away as well leaving Charles's sister, Margaret, a widow as well. She and I have become close: Margaret and I chat on the phone and by email and Facebook. We have many experiences to share and can laugh and weep as appropriate. His brother, Joel, passed away recently. His loss is a deeply felt and personal one to my children and me.

My sister, Jill, is in Rochester, NY where she is a Process Excellence Manager/Master Black Belt with Ortho Clinical Diagnostics while my sister, Sherry, retired from her position as Director of Georgia Shares and has moved to Dover, DE to be near her daughter, Melissa, and grandchildren, Benjamin, Julianna, and Lillian. My other niece, Ginger, lives in Atlanta and works for the CDC.

Life moves on! Mark, Charlaine and I are a close family. When we add in their spouses, Jill and Adam, we become a gregarious bunch. But, adding Jackson to the mix just completes us. Charles would be so happy . . . and somewhere up there in heaven, he is happy. God is watching over us and we are safe and secure in His love.

Many days have been given over to counting my blessings:

God led me to Charles and bound us for life;

We overcame my illness with Tuberculosis;

Strengthened we made it through college and the seminary;

God led us to pastorates in eight wonderful churches;

God found us three marvelous children and facilitated their adoption;

We were led to a location that allowed me to go to college and get a teaching certificate to assure our children's education, and additional degrees to give me raises in pay while I taught—AND gave me the retirement pay that allows me to live comfortably today.

When Charles returned from Brazil stricken with cancer, God mercifully found the physicians we needed and took him quickly so that he did not linger and suffer;

Our children have found excellent spouses and careers that insure them of happy and long lives filled with love and security;

In one unexpected but miraculous gift, God gave us Jackson—the grandson I never would have believed that I could love as much as I love my children.

God saved my soul and gave me the Christian life that He promised through His son, Jesus Christ. The marvel of that astounds me every single day;

The fine people that we met and to whom we ministered throughout the years have added to my blessings in ways that words cannot describe; and,

With my soul's salvation, He has promised me eternity in heaven and that when I reach the Pearly Gates, I shall be able to praise my God forever.

Then too, I am thankful for each morning when open my eyes to behold the beauty of the sky, the trees, the mountains. There is JOY in every morning.

I would be remiss if I did not admit that in these years there have been many disappointments, opportunities that I missed because I was not in tune with God, hurts that could have only been healed by God Himself, hours and hours of plain out old hard work that left me so fatigued that I was not really sure who I was, things that made me think, "Why am I doing this? Is this life really worth it?" Answers, aid, assistance, understanding and compassion always came to me from God Himself, though He used many of His children to people my life and help me stay centered when I was off center. He used many women who taught me strength, power, and hope. For all of the disappointments and hurts, there have been tenfold golden shining moments when I could feel His presence with me, leading me, taking the pain, the hurt, and all of that from me.

So, when I look at my Pastor's wife, I feel only love and gratitude to her for being who she is, for making a home for him and giving him a family, for trusting him, following him, and loving him. I pray for her every single solitary day. And when this Pastor leaves and a new one comes, that woman will be in my prayers and receive my love. We are, after all, Ruths in every sense of the word. Ruth did not give up because life was hard, or because she lost her husband, or because she was tired. She led a committed life. That is what we Pastors' Wives do. Just pray for us.

The knowledge that God led me into this life encourages me daily so that in valleys, on pinnacles and through every routine I can honestly say, "Don't make me leave you, for I want to go wherever you go, and to live wherever you live; your people shall be my people and your God, shall be my God . . . May the Lord do terrible things to me if I allow anything but death to separate us" (Ruth 1:16 thru 17 TLB). True, I have lost my husband, my Pastor, my mate; but, I have not lost my call. God speaks to me today as He did all of those years ago. He must still have something for me to do: I am still here, and I listen for His call just as I did when I was sixteen. Without Him I can do nothing, But with Him "I can do all things through Him who strengthens me" (Philippians 4:13 TLB).

That is my prayer today.

Truly, my name is Ruth, it's just that the wayfarers on this road have changed to only God and me. The mission has not changed. The relationship has not changed. I will do whatever God wants, be who He wants, and live as He leads me. That plan has served me well for my entire life, and will take me onward into eternity.

At this stage of my life, I often think about the time when my life shall end and I shall enter the Pearly Gates. Confident that I have much for which to account, I can only say to Him, "I have fought the good fight; I have finished the race; I have kept the faith (2 Timothy 4:7).

My prayer is that when that time comes, I shall meet my Maker and He will say to me, "Well done, thou good and faithful servant" (Matthew 25:21).

From the Author

Thank you for reading my little book. I hope that you have found some thread of joy in it and that you know that I am praying that you too find God's will for your life. Truly, living in the center of His will is the greatest blessing life can afford.

If you are not a Christian, I urge you to read the following scriptures and allow God to speak to you. As you repent of your sins and accept His love and forgiveness freely, your joy shall be multiplied. His plan is simple:

A – "For all have sinned and come short of the glory of God" (Romans 3:23 KJV). This means that God realizes that you are not perfect nor does He expect you to be. He understands that because we are human, we sin. Because He understands who you are TODAY, He does not have to wait for you to earn his forgiveness. He knows your sins.

B – "Believe on the Lord Jesus Christ and thou shalt be saved" (Acts 16:31 KJV). This means that the first thing that you have to do is believe in God's son, Jesus Christ who died for your sins. The blood that Jesus shed on the cross washes away all of your sins.

Simply believing in His love brings you God's salvation. Think about this. Right where you are this moment, you have only to believe and your soul is saved for eternity. Is that not amazing? God does not make you jump through hoops or earn your salvation. He gives it to you in return for your recognizing your sinless state and accepting His Son. The choice could not be simpler.

C – "Confess with your mouth that Jesus is Lord and believe in your heart that God raised Him from the dead, you will be saved." (Romans 10:9 NLB). This means that after you have believed in Jesus, you have only to let it be known of your belief. This means that while you are accepting and believing that Jesus is God's son and that He was raised from the dead, you must confess it. That means tell others. Share your news. Go to your church and tell your Pastor. In other words, "Don't be ashamed!"

Then, you simply pray the Sinner's prayer.

"God, I know that I am a sinner. I know that I deserve the consequences of my sin. However, I am trusting in Jesus Christ as my Savior. I believe that His death and resurrection provided for my forgiveness. I trust in Jesus, and Jesus alone, as my personal Lord and Savior. Thank you God for saving me and forgiving me! Amen"

Now, if you have made the three steps above and truly pray this prayer, God will not only hear you, but will answer you with total forgiveness and walk with you for the rest of your life until you meet Him in heaven.

I am praying for you today that you will join the great host of us who have made this decision and count ourselves as His children.

God bless you.

If you are in the area, I personally invite you to come and worship with us at McConnell Memorial Baptist Church in Hiawassee, Georgia and at Friendship Baptist Church in Hiawassee, Georgia. You will find a welcome, fellowship, and the presence of God.

Contact me at

https://www.grendelb@windstream.net